The Complete Guide to
Growing Your Own Hops, Malts, and Brewing Herbs:
Everything You Need to Know
Explained Simply

John Peragine

THE COMPLETE GUIDE TO GROWING YOUR HOPS, MALTS, AND BREWING HERBS: EVERYTHING YOU NEED TO KNOW EXPLAINED SIMPLY

Library of Congress Cataloging-in-Publication Data

Peragine, John N., 1970-
  The complete guide to growing your own hops, malts, and brewing herbs : everything you need to know explained simply / by: John Peragine.
     p. cm.
  Includes bibliographical references and index.
  ISBN-13: 978-1-60138-353-2 (alk. paper)
  ISBN-10: 1-60138-353-3 (alk. paper)
  1. Hops. 2. Grain. 3. Malt. 4. Herbs. 5. Brewing--Equipment and supplies. I. Title.
  SB317.H64P47 2010
  633.8'2--dc22
                          2010029671

INTERIOR DESIGN: Rhana Gittens • ASSISTANT EDITOR: Molly Bruce
COVER DESIGN: Meg Buchner • meg@megbuchner.com
BACK COVER DESIGN: Jacqueline Miller • millerjackiej@gmail.com

Printed on Recycled Paper

Printed in the United States

We recently lost our beloved pet "Bear," who was not only our best and dearest friend but also the "Vice President of Sunshine" here at Atlantic Publishing. He did not receive a salary but worked tirelessly 24 hours a day to please his parents. Bear was a rescue dog that turned around and showered myself, my wife, Sherri, his grandparents Jean, Bob, and Nancy, and every person and animal he met (maybe not rabbits) with friendship and love. He made a lot of people smile every day.

We wanted you to know that a portion of the profits of this book will be donated to The Humane Society of the United States. *–Douglas & Sherri Brown*

The human-animal bond is as old as human history. We cherish our animal companions for their unconditional affection and acceptance. We feel a thrill when we glimpse wild creatures in their natural habitat or in our own backyard.

Unfortunately, the human-animal bond has at times been weakened. Humans have exploited some animal species to the point of extinction.

The Humane Society of the United States makes a difference in the lives of animals here at home and worldwide. The HSUS is dedicated to creating a world where our relationship with animals is guided by compassion. We seek a truly humane society in which animals are respected for their intrinsic value, and where the human-animal bond is strong.

Want to help animals? We have plenty of suggestions. Adopt a pet from a local shelter, join The Humane Society and be a part of our work to help companion animals and wildlife. You will be funding our educational, legislative, investigative and outreach projects in the U.S. and across the globe.

Or perhaps you'd like to make a memorial donation in honor of a pet, friend or relative? You can through our Kindred Spirits program. And if you'd like to contribute in a more structured way, our Planned Giving Office has suggestions about estate planning, annuities, and even gifts of stock that avoid capital gains taxes.

Maybe you have land that you would like to preserve as a lasting habitat for wildlife. Our Wildlife Land Trust can help you. Perhaps the land you want to share is a backyard—that's enough. Our Urban Wildlife Sanctuary Program will show you how to create a habitat for your wild neighbors.

So you see, it's easy to help animals. And The HSUS is here to help.

THE HUMANE SOCIETY
OF THE UNITED STATES.

2100 L Street NW • Washington, DC 20037 • 202-452-1100
www.hsus.org

Dedication

I dedicate this book to one of my oldest friends Mike and his family; also to Wendy, Daniel, Chaney, Blaine, and Avin. If we had known how to make beer back then, we would have been gods.

Table of Contents

Chapter 3:
Working With Other Grains   93

Chapter 4:
Hops
135

Chapter 5:
Brewing Herbs
163

Chapter 6:
Culture Your Own Yeast
181

Chapter 7:
The Essentials of Home Brewing   203

Chapter 8:
Home Brewing Extract
with Specialty Grains   249

Appendix D: Malt Types and Uses   307

Bibliography   311

Glossary   317

Author Biography   329

Index   331

Introduction

"Beer is living proof that God loves us and wants us to be happy."
— *Benjamin Franklin, one of founding fathers of the United States*

T his is the best quote I can think of that describes the wonders of beer. Throughout my life, I have tried beers from around the world, and I never get tired of tasting them. There are so many diverse and tasty variations that I can only hope to continue my search for new and exciting beer offerings. Since beginning this hobby — obsession — I have come to appreciate what goes into creating even the simplest of beers. Our ancestors were chemical and culinary geniuses to have come up with not only the concept of beer, but also the perfection of the practice of creating it.

These ancient people created the first beers at home and, therefore, were the original home brewers. They figured out a way to boil grains, such as barley, until the grains released fermentable sugars. This produced a sticky, sweet liquid known as **wort**. They allowed this wort to be fermented by wild yeasts that exist everywhere in nature; these yeasts convert the sugar into alcohol and the carbon dioxide into the bubbles found in beer. Later, these beer pioneers began adding other plants to give these simple beers more flavor and body. They used herbs such as heather and — more recently — added the plants called **hops**. This process of fermenting barley and adding bitter hops creates what we now know as **ale**.

Whether you are new to home brewing or are a veteran, there are a number of reasons why growing your own ingredients at home is beneficial to the home brewer: You have total control over what goes into your beer and what does not. You have the ability to create completely organic beers based upon the type of gardening techniques you choose. An organic beer is created with ingredients that have been grown without the use of artificial fertilizers, herbicides, and pesticides, and making your own is possible because you will know exactly what is going into your beer. You will be in control from seed to suds. If you are a home brewer, or are thinking about becoming one, here are just some of the benefits to creating your own beer garden:

1. There are good-tasting beers, and there are bad-tasting beers. But what if you could create a *better*-tasting beer? You can concoct a satisfying beer using a beer kit or store-bought ingredients, but you can create a significantly superior beer when using your own ingredients. A beer kit contains all of the ingredients, such as barley malt, hops, and yeast, that you will need to create a home brew, but it uses premeasured ingredients. By creating yours from scratch, using the step-by-step instructions in this book, you will be using the best ingredients, because they are the freshest, highest-quality ingredients you can find. You can feel motivated to create the best, most memorable beer

possible when you are cutting, drying, and preparing your ingredients from scratch.

2. You can grow ingredients that you may not be able to find readily available anywhere else — specialty grains, unique types of hops, or unusual herbs that you can pull fresh from your garden and drop into a boiling pot of brew. **Specialty grains** are grains that add color and flavors, which add more depth to a beer but often are not fermentable grains. They are added during the boiling process that creates the wort. An example of a specialty grain is a black patent malt. This **malt** is dark and adds color and a chocolaty flavor that is distinctive in stout beers. Malt is produced when grain, and in this case barley, is allowed to sprout. This releases sugars that can then be broken down by yeast during fermentation.

    Some hops are used to add bitterness to a beer. These are added early on in the brewing process as heat converts enzymes in the hops to create a bitter flavor. Examples of hops used to add bitterness are green bullet, herald, and horizon. Some hops are added later on for aroma. Examples of aroma hops are Aquila, Bramling Cross, and Challenger. *Many different species of hops will be discussed in Chapter 4.* Each hop adds a different level of aroma and bitterness to a beer. In addition to hops, herbs such as hyssop, juniper, and lavender are used to create unique flavors and aromas in a home brew. In addition, the cost of creating beer using your own ingredients is substantially cheaper. Can you believe that you can make about 6 gallons of your own beer for what it would cost to buy a six-pack of your favorite commercial beer? *Chapter 6 allows you to take an even greater level of control by teaching you how to culture yeasts yourself for home brewing.* This can drop the cost of your brew even further.

3. You will understand how beer is made and learn more about its evolution. This opens up all kinds of avenues for exploration and experimentation, and allows you to create historical beers, such as Chimay Trappist beer that has been produced by Trappist monks in Belgium for more than 300 years, and use herbs like anise, a licorice-flavored herb that is not commonly used in commercial beers. These can create some unique libations.

4. The process is genuinely fun. Home brewing is an exciting hobby on its own, but combine it with gardening and chemistry, and it is fun, exciting, and a great learning experience. Both home brewing and gardening require patience, intelligence, and an independent, experimental spirit. You may find that it will never get dull because the combination of ingredients will be endless. Each batch will be a handcrafted, unique creation that can impress friends, family, and even judges at beer competitions.

This book is about growing all the ingredients you will need to create a beer in your kitchen, with the exception of adjuncts such as additional sugar used to increase carbonation in the beer. You will also learn about the steps in the process and the necessary equipment involved in brewing your own beer. *If you are adventurous, then in Chapter 6 you will learn how to cultivate your own yeast strains for home brew use.*

One of the aspects about home brewing that is so exciting is the amount of control over that final beer a home brewer has. Unfortunately, a home brewer can be confined by the hops that are available, the types of malt and grains he or she can purchase from a home-brew shop, and any other flavor additives that a home brewer may wish to add to a brew that are available for purchase. But what if you could go one step further and control the outcome from the beginning?

Although this book contains some brewing techniques and recipes, its focus is on controlling the beer-making process from the beginning: growing the ingredients in your own garden. Various combinations of grains, hops, and herbs can be used to create just about any beer you can taste commercially and even allow you to create new ones that you might never have considered.

With the ingredients growing in your backyard, you can decide to make a lager, an apricot wheat, or even a triple-strength IPA (India pale ale). You will learn how to grow grains, hops, and herbs from seed and rhizome, harvest these ingredients, and store them. Grains have to undergo a special process called "malting" in order to be used in the creation of beer, and this malting process will be broken down easily in this book to help you replicate the brewing process used by the big breweries — right in your own kitchen.

Hops and herbs must be dried and stored in a special way. Step-by-step instructions take you from planting to harvesting, drying, and storage. You will have all the instructions you need to create many styles of beer at home easily and successfully, whether you are a beginning home brewer, advanced home brewer, or a gardener who wants to create a one-of-a-kind brewing garden.

For the beginning home brewer, Chapter 8 describes the process of using the ingredients you have grown in your backyard to create a beer that your friends and family will rave about. For the more experienced home brewers, there are more unusual herbs, such as bee balm, and uncommon beer grains, such as amaranth. It is time to put your gardening gloves on, and create your unique beer garden.

Chapter 1

The Components of a Beer Garden

"The mouth of a perfectly happy man is filled with beer."
— Egyptian proverb

A vast number of fermentable drinks exists that humans can create: beer, wine, liquor, cider, and mead, to name a few. Every one of these beverages has one thing in common: a fermentable sugar as its base. For beer, the sugar that is converted by yeast into ethanol — alcohol — is derived from grains. When most people in the United States think about beer, they usually imagine lagers. Coors, Budweiser, and other light-yellow lagers are mostly mild tasting, have almost no hop flavor or bitterness to them, and are actually based upon a beer type called a Czech pilsner. These American lager beers are made with corn and rice added as adjunct grains; the central fermentable grain is barley, but these types of beers have a very light barley malt taste to them.

In reality, American lager beers are a little trickier to make than ales. This book will focus on European or early American-style ales, which include a lighter pale ale, all the way to a dark-chocolate stout. The dark chocolate refers to the rich flavor and dark color — not because any actual chocolate is actually added to it, although there are commercial breweries that do add actual chocolate, such as Young's Double Chocolate Stouts and Rogue Brewery's Chocolate Stout. As you will learn while growing, kilning, and eventually roasting your own grains, the maltiness and color of a beer depend largely on the degree to which you roast the barley malt.

Grain is the body of your beer garden. You will need about 800 square feet in order to produce enough grain to make either five 5-gallon full-grain recipes, which means you will use all of the grain from your garden to produce each batch, or about 30 partial-grain batches, which means you will be using premade malt extract for part of the home-brew recipe. You can plant them in squares or in rows and plant other herbs and hops around them or in the center part of your garden. Certain varieties of barley, such as easy-thresh hulless barley, can grow as high as 3 feet tall.

Barley is one of the earliest cultivated grains known in the history of man. The ancient Assyrians, Egyptians, and people who lived around the Mediterranean region of the world have been growing barley as a food staple for thousands of years. In Europe, barley was used as the main component in bread until about the 16th century, when it was replaced with wheat and potatoes.

Let us now look at the skeletal structure of the beer garden: the hops. Hops give beer the bitterness you may have experienced in ales that you can buy from the store or from your local microbrew pub. Hops are the skeletal part of your garden, growing high up on a trellis system. The trellis system is a series of poles that hop vines are trained up; a traditional trellis system uses wires strung between poles at the end of rows. This allows more hop plants to be planted and gives a greater yield and more control over the height to which these plants grow, which is important during harvesting season so that you can reach your hops without the need for a cherry picker machine. A cherry picker is much like the bucket on the top of a fire truck; it extends by the use of a telescopic pole. These trellis systems are higher than the herbs, and so different herbs can be planted between the hop trellises or at the end of the rows. You can plant four or more rows of hops to get a good yield. When looking at a beer garden, these hop trellis will look like a skeleton that pokes through the canvas of grain and herbs.

You can either create the trellis in the center of your garden in a box-like formation, or you can use them to create a fence that keeps critters out of the rest of your beer garden inside. You can also create a three-dimensional look with your trellis by placing it at the back of your garden; then you can plant high herbs and grains and, finally, herbs that create a ground cover. This not only looks great, but it also can make your garden easier to manage.

There are some space considerations when planting hops. Hops are planted in what is referred to as a **hop yard**. The area should have full sun exposure and good air circulation. Most hop varieties prefer direct sun to mature. Hops are planted in small hills that are spaced between two and a half and three feet apart (.8 to 1 meter), with one to two **rhizomes** in each hill. A rhizome is the name of the horizontal stem of a hop plant. A rhizome is planted underground, where it sends out roots and shoots from its nodes. **Nodes** are the part of the plant that contains the hop buds and will grow into cones that are the part of the plant used in home brewing. *This book will take you step-by-step through growing your own hops; see Chapter 4 to learn more about hops.*

Finally, there is the green skin of your garden: beer herbs. Hops are actually relatively new to the beer-making scene; the first ancient brewers used herbs and other plants instead of hops to give their beers a little depth and character. Though no one is exactly sure, it was not until the 14th century that hops were used in breweries in Germany. In about the 16th century, hops were introduced into English beer, although they were not readily accepted at first.

Before there were hops in beer, people used other plants to give beer unique flavors as well as preserve beer from spoilage and flavor decay. The original term of "ale" that was used in Europe prior to 1300 referred to beer with no hops. Before hops, brewers would use a "beer gruit," which was a mixture of herbs and spices in beer that included mint, chamomile, burnet, betony, marjoram, wild thyme, rosemary, sage, and elder flowers. Herbs were added to beer after the **primary fermentation**, which refers to the vigorous bubbling caused by yeast transforming sugars into alcohol and carbon dioxide. Today, this technique of adding hops after primary fermentation is referred to as **dry hopping**. At other times, herbs were added to beer after the beer was finished and were steeped in the ale much like a tea before it was drank.

There are British breweries that used ginger and licorice in their ales until just 40 years ago, and in Belgium, there are many specialty beers that still contain different combinations and beer recipes that contain various garden herbs. You can use store-bought dry and fresh herbs to create unique herbal beers. There are differences between dried and fresh herbs, because they react differently in brewing. However, it can be more difficult to find uncommon herbs such as anise hyssop or borage in a grocery store. This is why growing and even drying your own herbs gives you fresher herbs and more varieties to experiment with. *You will learn more about what these beer herbs are, how to grow them, and how to use them in Chapter 5.*

Creating your own brew garden can be plenty of fun — and very rewarding. It will cost less to grow and process the grains, hops, and herbs at home, than it would to buy the prepared ingredients at a local or online home-brew supply store. Once the garden is established, it can produce ingredients for many years — and many gallons of beer — to come. Here are some comparisons in prices of commercial beers and home-brew beers.

Guinness Stout Price Comparison

A six-pack of 12 ounce-bottles of Guinness Stout retails for about $9. There are 128 fluid ounces in a gallon, and most home-brew recipes and kits create 5 gallons of beer per batch. There are approximately nine six-packs in a 5-gallon batch of beer. Therefore, it would cost about $81, plus bottle deposits and tax to buy 5 gallons of Guinness Stout. This breaks down to about $1.50 per bottle of beer.

Also, look into the price of a home-brew kit. An Irish stout beer kit from **homebrewmart.com** costs $45. If you have your own equipment and used bottles, this breaks down to about 83 cents per bottle of beer. It is fresh and made by your own hands. But, though you may not pay taxes and bottle deposits on your beer kit, if you order online, you will have to pay shipping, which varies according to where you live. If you buy the kit at a local beer shop, you will have to pay federal and state taxes on the kit.

If you make beer from your garden, however, you will save substantially more money. Here, we will break down what it might cost you. It is assumed you have your home-brew supplies in the calculation. If you do not, the average cost to purchase all the supplies needed is about $60 — but you will only need to make this purchase once. If you make multiple batches of beer, then the cost can be spread out over time.

Take, for example, the following recipe for an all-grain beer. This type of recipe uses grain that has not been processed, such as the kind of grain you would grow in your garden. The different types of malts listed refer to the type of roast that is used on the barley. *You will learn how to roast grain in Chapter 2.* The names of the hops refer to the variety of hops used. Below is the cost of each item purchased separately. The prices are adjusted to create this particular recipe, because you have to buy larger amounts than you will need. For instance, a 2-ounce bag of Clusters hops costs $4.50, but you only need 1 ounce to create a 5-gallon recipe. You can use what is left over in another batch.

- 11 lbs. pale malt $17.60
- 1 lb. British crystal malt $1.60
- 0.5 lb. black patent malt $0.80 cents
- 0.5 lb. roast barley $0.80 cents
- 1 oz. Clusters hops $2.25
- 0.5 oz. Willamette hops $1.40
- 0.5 oz. EKG hops $1.00

- London ale yeast $9.95
- 0-40 cc lactic acid (88% solution) to finished beer (to taste) $4.75 (2 oz.)

Total cost = $40.15, or 74 cents per bottle

When you grow barley, you can turn it into any type of malt you choose through kilning and roasting. Suppose you want to grow a 20 by 40 foot (6 by 12 meters) bed of grain. That will yield up to a bushel of grain, or 47 pounds (21 kilograms). This recipe requires a total of 13 pounds of grain, or about a quarter of the plot's yield. It takes 5 pounds of seed to grow in a 20 by 40 foot (6 by 12 meters) plot of grain. An average price for barley is about $1 a pound, so it would cost $5 to grow an 800-square-foot (74 meters squared) plot. In other words, you will use $1.25 worth of grain.

A hop plant can yield 2 pounds of dry hops. Because there are at least three different types of hops used in this recipe, you will need three hops plants.

Rhizomes cost about $5.25 each. You only need .50 ounces of Willamette hops, so the cost for this recipe would be about 8 cents' worth of hops. You would need 16 cents' worth of clusters hops and 8 cents' worth of EKG hops.

You can use an **all-grain** recipe to produce a stout beer similar to Guinness. All-grain means that you are using grains instead of malt extracts found in beer kits. **Malt extracts** are in liquid or powdered form and are processed to remove water from the pure malt. When the malt extract is added to the beer, it is reconstituted when it is exposed to water again. It is very similar to frozen orange juice concentrate you can buy in the frozen food section at a grocery store. When you add water to the concentrate, it becomes orange juice again. Thus, the total cost for making Irish stout beer using ingredients from your beer garden and using an all-grain recipe is

- grain $1.25
- hops $0.32
- yeast $9.95
- lactic acid $4.75

Total cost = $16.27 for a 5-gallon batch, or $0.30 a bottle.

Summary for 5 gallons of Irish stout beer

- Guinness Stout retail: $81, or $1.50 a bottle
- beer kit: $45, or 83 cents a bottle
- all-grain recipe: $40.15, or 74 cents a bottle
- beer garden all-grain recipe: $16.27, or 30 cents a bottle

Furthermore, herbs and other brewing plants can make a beautiful and unique kitchen garden — more interesting than what you might expect even a chef to use. Many of the herbs mentioned in this book will flourish and bloom as visually appealing flowers, and you can enjoy this garden of a multitude of colors, depending on the herbs you choose. You will not need a huge farm, but you will need some dedicated garden space. There are different space requirements needed for grains, herbs, and hops, and the amount of space you will need depends largely upon what and how much of each plant you intend to grow. Each chapter will give you the specific dimensions you will need to grow the different plants you can choose from. Obviously, the more room you have, the more you can grow. If you intend to grow hops, be aware that you will need ample vertical space to build a trellis system. Hops are vines that need to grow upward in order for the maximum light exposure, maintenance, and ease of harvesting; a **trellis** provides support and a direction for these hop vines to grow. You can also grow herbs in empty spots around the yard, although some may need specific water, soil, and sunlight. *The specific needs of each herb will be explained in Chapter 5.*

Materials

Each ingredient will require slightly different materials. Hops, for example, require that you have a tall, sturdy trellis system and purchase hop rhizomes. **Rhizomes** are roots that look like a skinny ginger root, a small potato, or even a twig. They are plant- ed in the ground, and the vines grow upward along your trellis. You will need to look for hop rhizomes at specialty stores, like Northwest Hops in Hubbard, Oregon (**www.northwesthops. com**). Rhizomes must be planted in the spring between March and mid-June, depending on your climate. You may have to use a few different companies to look for more varieties, because one company will not have all of the different rhizomes available. It is also a good idea to call the company before purchasing your hops because different hops varieties have different climate needs. *In Appendix B, there are number of resources to purchase rhizomes from.*

Grains will require that you work the land with specific tools and buy seed. You will need to be able to till the earth either by hand or a small gas tiller. The seed you will need to purchase from grain seed suppliers. *Appendix B has a list of these suppliers.*

Each herb needs its own unique growing conditions or additional supplies to help it flourish. Common herbs like lavender or basil can be purchased as seeds or small seedlings at most landscape or garden supply stores, and are usually available in early spring. Some plants, such as dandelion, can be harvested in the wild, although you should make sure they have not been sprayed with fertilizers, pesticides, or herbicides. These chemicals can find their way into your beer, and although they might not make you ill at such low amounts, they can cause your beer to have an off taste. You may have to do a more in-depth search for uncommon varieties, such as gentian or clary sage. *Use the resources provided in Appendix C.*

The other materials you will need are typically found in most gardens:

- 100-foot hose and nozzle sprayer to water your plants. Your hose needs to be long enough to reach the farthest plants in your garden. You can also use a drip irrigation system; however, this can take some work and digging to set up, although it has the advantage of keeping your plants well watered, and it does not waste water. A drip irrigation kit in the size you would need to water hops, grain, and herbs runs about $91. *You can look in Appendix B for some resources if you cannot find them at the local landscaping or gardening store.*

- Small garden hoe. You can find these at most local gardening supply stores. This is what you will use to dig up weeds and loosen the ground before planting seeds, rhizomes, or seedlings.

- Shovel. An average-sized shovel will do. You will need to dig holes for seedlings and to build your trellis system.

- Small gas-powered tiller. The tiller loosens the dirt and gets rid of weeds in order to do spring planting. It can replace a hoe for weeding purposes as long as the space between the rows is wide enough to accommodate the tiller. Try buying the smallest power tiller possible; they are easier to push and manage in a tight garden space.

- Post-hole digger. This tool is almost essential to create holes to place the poles into for your trellis system. It is more difficult to just rely on a shovel for this job. Post-hole diggers can be a little expensive (about $38), so you might ask around and borrow one.

- Garden shears. Shears are used to prune all the plants in your garden. If you buy large hedge clippers, you can use these to cut the grains when they are ready for harvesting. Small pruning shears can be helpful for cutting hops, excess foliage, and herbs when they are ready to be harvested.

- Gloves. Gloves protect your hands while you are working in the garden and give you a better grip when pulling weeds.

- Rake. This tool will keep your garden tidy. Once you pull up weeds, it is a good idea to rake them and remove them from your garden to prevent them from re-rooting or spreading more seeds to grow.

- Yardstick. This tool is handy for measuring out your garden space, as well as measuring the space between the rows and the height of your plants, which can indicate that it is time to harvest them.

- Twine. You will need strong twine to allow the hops to grab on and grow upward. In addition, you can stake down twine when you measure out plots in order to see the plots when you are planting them. This will help you organize and plot out your garden space.

In Chapter 7, you will find that you will need additional tools to build a hop trellis or pole. Once you buy most of these materials, you will need to buy a minimal amount of supplies year to year to keep your hobby beer garden going.

Time

Like any other garden, it takes time for plants to grow in a beer garden. The process of planting, growing, harvesting, and preparing the plot for next year's harvest takes the entire year. The best time to start planting your garden is in early spring. Once planted, it takes about three to four months for your garden to mature and be ready to harvest; thus, you need some patience. Some herbs will have to be sown in late autumn, since they require being in the ground for a winter before they will grow. Sowing seeds means planting them in the ground. You will need to plan ahead, because it will not be until the next summer that they will be ready for harvesting.

This does not mean you have to wait for the fun to begin. You can use this time for choosing your beer recipes, researching what plants you want to grow and when you need to plant them, creating garden plots on paper so you have an idea of what your garden will look like, and even talking to other farmers about what plants grow best in your climate.

Location and Timing

Knowing whether certain plants will grow where you live could take some research on your part. You will need a sunny place for your hops and a well-drained area for your grains. A well-drained area allows water to drain away from the soil as opposed to ground that is soggy or swampy. Different herbs require different environments, soil, and climate. Fortunately, a number of resources exist to provide you information on what plants can grow in your particular location.

- Call your local cooperative extension office of the U.S. Department of Agriculture. These are usually located with other county offices. Their extension agents and master gardeners are there to help farmers and gardeners, so use their services and connections. The office can offer the best resources when it comes to climate, soil, and water issues, and they can help you choose the right varieties of plants for your beer garden.

- Try your local gardening center. This does not mean the garden center from a large home-and-garden chain — look for a local greenhouse, nursery, or garden center. Not only can the employees give you advice about what will grow locally, but they also might have the plants that you need ready for transplanting. They can also have the tools you will need to make the coolest beer garden on the planet.

- Visit a local **farmers market**. A farmers market is a meeting place of local farmers who set up booths to sell produce, plants, and even seeds from their garden. These are usually small farms, but you can find a lot of different plants and seeds, especially beer herbs for your garden. These often take place in a park-  ing lot once a week, or they can be events hosted in more permanent structures. These can function like garden centers, except they usually have other indispensable experts — farmers. They might lend equipment, give you advice, or even have materials, such as unkilned grain that you can use. At the same time, the local farmers provide you with garden-fresh ingredients. You might even be able to pick herbs and harvest grain on their farms; it rarely hurts to ask. Furthermore, the experience of volunteering on a working farm under the supervision of a veteran farmer can be priceless.

- Ask for advice from your local home-brew shop. A home-brew shop is a store that sells equipment and ingredients to make homemade beer and, sometimes, homemade wine. *If you cannot find a home-brew shop in your area, a list of home-brew shops you can buy supplies and materials from online is included in Appendix B.* Shops may even have hop rhizomes for sale, which can cut out some of the guess-work, because they will be selling varieties that will grow in your area. Even if they do not have experience growing beer ingredients, they are experts in brewing beer and can be a great resource.

- Along with the last resource, you might be able to find a local home-brew club or organization. You can find if you have a local home-brew association by checking online and typing in your city along with the phrase "home-brew club." Numerous people involved with these clubs may be growing their own beer gardens. These are good opportunities to try out your own brew creations for feedback and try other home brewers' beers as well. This can provide inspiration and ideas for your own methods. You can also work with other home brewers and create a community garden or beer garden co-op in which you can share your garden harvest and trade to get some of theirs.

Community Home-brew Garden

Here are some steps in creating a community garden in which home brewers can work together to grow grain, hops, and herbs for home brewing purposes:

1.   **Get the brewers together.**

It takes time and planning to get a community garden together. You must find enough people willing to work on a home-brew garden to make it work. You can contact other local home brewers through home-brew clubs, or put up flyers at home-brew shops or even microbreweries where home brewers can often be found. Find a place to meet and invite the interested parties; then, begin to plan your garden. You will need to determine what you want to plant, where you want to plant, and who has garden tools. Each person can choose a plot in the garden and be responsible for the materials such as seeds and plants in their plot. Each member would then be responsible for weeding, planting, and harvesting his or her plot.

2.   **Find a garden spot.**

This can be a little tougher to do. Once you have decided what you want to plant and how much room you will need, you will need to find the land to work. If you are lucky, one of the people in your co-op will have some land to offer. If not, you can ask the city or county you live in if they have any land you might use as a community garden. Also, check local universities or colleges, because they often have available plots of land and would love volunteers to work the land and create a nice looking garden spot. Once you have a plot of land you are interested in, you need to check it out to make sure it is the right place for the types of grain, hops, and herbs you want to grow. You can take some soil samples and send them to an agricultural extension office in your county or to a soil-testing site. *See the options mentioned in Appendix B.* Be certain that you have access to water for your plot.

3.   **Figure out when to plant.**

Once you have the land, you must decide when to begin planting. Some herbs must be planted in the fall, while the majority of other herbs, grains, and hops must be planted in the spring. The members of your co-op must order their plants and be ready to plant their mini crops at the appropriate time. When figuring out where in the garden a particular person's plot is going to be, you need to consider things such as sun exposure and trellis building for the hops. It is better if each of the different types of plants is planted together. This makes the garden look more organized, encourages pollination of the pants, and makes it easier to maintain.

4.   **Make cleaning, building, and tilling days.**

Once you have decided where the plots are and when planting will begin, you will need to plan a day of cleaning the site. You will want to remove any debris, trash, and rocks that may get in the way. You will also want to plan a day of tilling the garden and a day of trellis building. All of these activities can take place on the same day, but planning is essential, and you want to make sure that you have the supplies, tools, and equipment you will need to build the garden. Once the garden is tilled, you should use twine and stakes to create the plot lines and create a map of the garden so that people know where their plots are. On the map, you should write the volunteers' names and what they are planting. You may also decide to erect a fence around your garden. This keeps animals and unwanted guests out of your garden. If you choose to use drip irrigation in your community beer garden, this would be the time to erect it. Also, if you are having mulch, fertilizer, or soil sent to you, it is a good idea to deliver this before you erect any trellises or fences, as these may be difficult to manage because of the weight and size of these items.

5.   **Get ready for opening day.**

This is a community garden you are building, so you will want the support of as much of the community as possible. You can have an official ribbon-cutting ceremony in which you invite friends, family neighbors, and even the press. You may find that with some publicity, you may have other volunteers come forward and offer to help you with your garden.

6.   **Plan tours.**

There will be people who become interested in your community beer garden as it grows. You should consider posting hours in which a volunteer can safely take visitors through your garden. You do not want people tramping through the garden without a guide. You may even decide to do home-brew demonstrations at certain times as well. This is a good way to get even more people to volunteer and help you with your beer garden.

> **7.**   **Harvest.**
>
> When it is time to harvest, you need to consider details, such as drying plants, kilning, and roasting grains. You can make a day or two of it. You can then split up the harvest among the members of the co-op and plan a brewing day.

It is best if you begin making your preparations during the autumn, because you can till the ground and let it rest. You can also place ground covering bought at a garden supply store to prevent weeds from taking root. This is also referred to as landscape fabric, and it comes in a roll. It is a thin material that you roll over your garden spot and stake down with metal stakes that are typically found in the same store section as the material. They look like large staples, and you can push them through the material into the ground with your foot. The material blocks out the sun while still allowing moisture to make its way to the ground. When it is time to plant, you can either pull the material up or make small holes in the material and plant seeds and seedlings. You can then place mulch on top of the ground cover, which makes an effective barrier against weeds.

Defending your garden from weeds is essential. Weeds compete for water and nutrients in the soil and can block the sun from young seedlings. They can take over a garden and make it hard to manage, and this can lead to plants dying and being choked out.

In the early spring, you can begin working the areas and deciding where the best light exposure is in your garden for the different plants you wish to plant. In each of the following chapters, you will learn the specifics of light, water, and space considerations for your grain, hops, and herbs.

Chapter 2

Grains and Malt

"Without question, the greatest invention in the history of mankind is beer. Oh, I grant you the wheel was also a fine invention, but the wheel does not go nearly as well with pizza."
— **Dave Barry, humor columnist**

Grains are the sugar base of any beer, and they contain the nutrients for yeast to convert those sugars into alcohol and carbon dioxide. This occurs through the process of simple **fermentation**. In addition to fermentable sugars, grains also provide taste and **body** to some types of wine. Body refers to the depth of taste; plain water would be considered to have very little body, whereas a milk shake might be considered to have plenty of body. It can also refer to the consistency of flavor. A full-bodied beer tastes consistent from the time you first taste it, until you swallow. A beer with little body may taste good at first taste, but may seem flat or have other off-flavors the longer it is in your mouth. The most common grain used in beers is barley.

Barley is a type of cereal grain derived from grass and is the fourth-largest cereal crop grown in the world, with a history of cultivation that stretches back centuries. There are three types of barley: two-row, four-row, and six-row. These numbers refer to the number of kernels located on each shaft of the grass. For brewing purposes, only the two-row and the six-row types are used. The two-row type of barley is thought to be superior, while the six-row has smaller kernels and higher protein content. Two-row barley creates a beer with a more full-bodied taste. But plenty of good-quality beers can be made from both types of barley.

When barley is harvested, it is sorted, dried, cleaned, and stored. This is preparation for the malting process in which sugars are transformed in the kernels. The process begins with steeping the grain in room-temperature water until it gains about 50 per-  cent of its original weight in water. Once this is done, the grain is then drained and, in commercial beer making, is placed in what is called a germination room. *You will learn more about this process later in Chapter 3.*

Once the barley is placed in the germination room, the germination or transformation of the grains occurs. **Germination** is the process in which the grain begins to grow shoots. During this germination process, the enzymes in the **aleurone** layer of the grain are released, creating new enzymes in the **endosperm** of the grain. The aleurone layer is the outer part of a grain, and the endosperm of the grain is the layer that surrounds the embryo of a seed and provides it food. Consider a kernel of corn. The outer yellow layer is the aleuronic. If you squeeze a kernel of corn, the embryo, which looks like a small seed, will come out. The material that is left inside the corn kernel is the endosperm.

Enzymes begin to break down the proteins and carbohydrates into simpler sugars, lipids, and amino acids, and they open up the starch reserves that exist to help the plant grow. Imagine that the starch is like small pebbles in a bag that exists in the endosperm of the grain. The enzymes rip open this bag and allow the starch to be released. This process is called **modification.**

These germination rooms are humidity-controlled, and the grains are turned and moved periodically in order to keep the grain bed temperature uniform. It is during this stage of germination that grain is called **green malt**.

Brewers can determine how much modification has occurred by the length of the **acrospire**, or plant shoot. The fully modified spire will be between 75 to 100 percent of the seed length. The trick is that the growth must be stopped, or the shoot will continue to grow — and the sugar that was created will be lost, because it will be used as food for the growth of the acrospire and, eventually, a seedling. A home brewer growing grain must watch this growth carefully.

After the grains begin to germinate, they are then placed in a **kiln** — a large, high-temperature oven — that slowly dries out the grains at a low temperature between 122 to 158 degrees Fahrenheit (50 to 70 degrees Celsius). In order to process grains at home, you will need to use a kiln. *At the end of Chapter 2, you will learn how to build a kiln at home.* This drying process stops the modification by destroying the enzymes, and it dries out grains to about 4 percent moisture. At this point, the grains are considered **base malt**, or are sometimes called **lager malt**. The lager malt is used to make lagers, which are usually a pale golden color. Lagers usually do not contain any other roasted grains that would make a darker color, which is often found in many types of ales.

The amount of starch conversion a grain has is referred to its **diastatic power.** Two-row barley may be preferred to six-row barley because it has a more refined flavor, fewer proteins, and a higher yield — the amount of malt it can create per pound — but six-row barley has a higher diastatic power, meaning it can create a heavier-bodied beer. This is what led to brewers thinning the beer by adding flavor adjuncts such as rice and corn. The rice and corn are adjuncts, which mean they do not add sugar for fermentation. These give the beer a smoother, lighter taste.

During the creation of beer, the brew maker must take on a process called **mashing**. This is done by adding boiling water to the grains; this activates enzymes that break the starches released during modification into fermentable sugars. This is the process used to create pale-colored malts, pilsner malts, and even malted wheat — the base fermentable sugars in most beers.

Pale malts are used in pale ales, bitter ales, and in the creation of other British beer malts. It is commonly used as base malt. Pale malts are kilned at lower temperatures in order to preserve all the brewing enzymes in the grain; this creates a beer that is light in color. Pilsner malt is used as the base of a pilsner lager and has a stronger flavor than pale malt. It is the lightest colored malt and is used in many American-style pilsner beers; it generally has a strong, sweet malt flavor.

In Britain, pilsner malts — or lager malts, as they are called there — are used to create golden ales, such as Munton's Lager Malt.

The Kölsch style beers in Germany also use a fair amount of pilsner malts. Examples of these style beers are Kölsch Ale made by Victory Brewing Company, Früh Kölsch made by Brauerei Früh Am Dom, Nodding Head Spring Ale made by Nodding Head Brewery, and Dragonmead Kaiser's Kölsch made by Dragonmead Microbrewery.

Malted wheat undergoes the same kilning process that barley does. Malted wheat is used in the German Hefeweizen style and the Belgian witbier style. In addition, lambic-style beers also use wheat as base malt. Examples of beers that use malted wheat are Weihenstephaner Hefeweissbier created by Brauerei Weihenstephan, Hoegaarden Brewery's witbier, and Framboise created by Lindemans.

Two different kinds of malts are used in beers: those that are mashed, and those that are not. Both types of malts start from the same grain, but are kilned and roasted further to create specific flavors and colors rather than adding more sugar for fermentation. You can easily make both types of malts at home.

Malts are further kilned and toasted to create special versions of malts, for example brown, black patent, Munich, and Vienna — each with a different flavor. The longer the grain is toasted and the higher the temperature, the darker and richer the flavored malts they will produce. The toasting process often destroys some of their **diastatic** power, so these versions are not used as a source of fermentable sugar in a beer and, hence, are not mashed in order release sugars for fermentation. The diastatic power, also referred to as the "diastatic activity" or "enzymatic power," is the grain's ability to break starches into smaller, simple sugars. Yeast needs these simple sugars, because it cannot process starches.

These are referred to as specialty malts, because these malts are added for flavor and color. Some of these malts undergo a special heating process that converts the starch in the hull into complex, yet unfermentable sugars. They are unfermentable because they are still in a form that yeast cannot process. These add a sweet taste to beer and are called **caramel** or crystal malts. These malts come in different degrees of roast and, therefore, color.

Depending on their color, they are given a color number referred to as a Lovibond, so often these malts are known by their **Lovibond** number, such as crystal 40 degrees Lovibond or crystal 60 degrees Lovibond. The higher the number, the darker the malt. The number is determined by comparison to a standardized color chart called the Lovibond comparator. This chart was created in Britain by the Tintometer Ltd. and invented by Joseph Lovibond in the 19th century. Tintometer® scales cost thousands of dollars; these are used commercially to determine the actual Lovibond number of a malt. But this is not necessary for the home brewer. A simple comparison chart like the one found at **http://kotmf. com/articles/color.php** can help you determine the Lovibond of a beer. *In Appendix C, you will see a list of malts and their corresponding Lovibond numbers.*

Besides these caramel-type malts, there are roasted malts such as chocolate 17 to 20 degrees Lovibond malt or black patent malt of 20 to 25 degrees Lovibond. These usually do not have any diastatic power left to them; they are just steeped in hot water to release their flavor and color characteristics.

In Chapter 3, you will learn more about the other class of grains, referred to as adjuncts. These are fermentable grains that are not barley. Some of the types of grains used are corn, rice, wheat, unmalted barley, and unmalted rye, which are used in some beers that require these extra types of grains. *In Chapter 3, some of the more common and interesting adjuncts will be explored.* You will learn how to grow, dry, and make use of these specialty grains in your beer.

With each type of preparation of the malts, a variety of different flavors can be created. *In Appendix C, you will find a list of different malts and the color and taste they can impart to a beer.* The following are the four main categories of malts used:

1. base malts
2. kilned-only malts
3. roasted-only malts
4. kilned and roasted malts

Each of these types of malts will vary in moisture, the time they are added to brew, and the temperature they need to be heated to when added to the brew, which is called wort during the brewing process. These characteristics will develop different flavors and colors in the beer.

Deciding What Type of Barley to Grow

Appendix B contains information about a number of different sources that sell grain. If you live in an area where it is typically grown, contact your local agricultural extension office about the best places to buy grain.

Your two main categories of barley to choose from are six-row and two-row. Keep in mind that the six-row varieties produce less malt extract that can be used in beer than two-row. Six-row does have the advantage of more naturally occurring enzymes that convert starches to fermentable sugar. Six-row is often better used with beer that uses adjuncts. Two-row malt creates less extract, but has fewer off-flavors that can occur from the grain hulls.

Consider the geographic location of your garden as one important factor to determine which type you use. Two-row barley grows better in milder climates than six-row barley does. Keep in mind that American varieties of two-row barley contain more enzymes for conversion than British varieties do. Two-row varieties of barley allow for more **tillering** — when the plant puts out more side shoots and, therefore, more grains. Two-row barley on a good year can produce three or four tillers on a single plant

Photo courtesy of USDA Natural Resources Conservation Service.

or, if it is not as good a year, only one or two. In a good year, the right amount of sun and rain exist with temperatures that do not fluctuate too much. This gives you more grains per square foot.

Most varieties of barley can grow easily in a home brewer's garden and are easier to grow than some of the other grains that are mentioned in the next chapter. This is because they do not require as much tending and are a hearty grain that can withstand longer periods of drought. Therefore, if you are planning on growing grains, consider starting with barley. Barley can be planted in late spring and has a rather short growing season, which means you can have a harvest quickly.

Barley grows well in a number of types of soils and rainfall levels, and, luckily, it grows the best in North America, because North America provides the best soil and climates that barley thrives in. Still, you should be careful in choosing the right variety, as some are more prone to **lodging**, a problem that occurs when grains fall over in clumps due to rain and wind.

Specific varieties of barley have been bred for the particular purpose of making beer. These varieties have been cultivated for many years, and new cultivars are being developed every year. A **cultivar** is a specific species of plant developed through deliberate selection or breeding. The newer varieties are better conditioned to grow in a wider variety of soil types and under different climate and moisture conditions. *Later in the chapter, you will learn the names of some of the newer cultivars, and the types that are most disease resistant.* Some of the older varieties have worked for brewers for centuries, so the choice is up to you. Again, do some research to see what types are being grown in your area and which varieties are the most successful.

You may notice that some of the barley may be referred to as **"hulled"** or **"hulless."** The hull is the outer layer of the barley. In order to remove the hull of a barley grain, commercial barley millers do a process called pearling. Having hulless, or "naked grains," eliminates the need for this process. The hulless grains actually do have a hull, but they are thin and fall off during harvesting. The hulless varieties were cultivated for their digestibility, especially in livestock, as the hull is harder for the stomach to process.

To get even more in depth, there are even different classifications of two- and six-row barley varieties. The following page has a chart with the different varieties of grain. The terms bearded, hulled, and color refer to the physical appearance of the different types of barley you can grow.

Six-row varieties of barley

Color of barley	Common six-rowed	True six-rowed	Hulled	Hulless	Beard	Beardless
Black	x		x	x	x	
White	x		x	x	x	x
		x	x		x	

Two-row varieties of barley

Heads	Bearded	Hulled	Hulless
Nodding heads	x	x	
Erect heads	x	x	x

These two tables represent all the different varieties of barley that are possible. In this list, you will notice the term "beard"; a beard on barley refers to the 3-inch-long awn — or bristle — that projects from the top of the plant. In contrast, beardless varieties do not have an awn. Some newer varieties that are in between are called hooded, which means they have a short awn.

The disadvantage to bearded varieties is that awns can be itchy and irritating to the skin when you work with them. But also keep in mind that an advantage to bearded barley is that it will repel deer, a common pest to barley — the awns can poke them in the eye if they are trying to eat the plant. Beards are a natural defense for barley. If you have trouble with animals eating your plants, then you might want to consider a bearded variety.

Here is a list of the common and easier varieties that home brewers can grow in their beer garden:

Name of grain	How long it takes to mature	Two-row or six-row	Height	Notes about particular variety
Excelsior	*90 days*	*Six-row*	*40 inches (102 cm)*	*Large, purple heads; little lodging; hand threshed; vigorous growth*
Two-row klages	*90 days*	*Two-row*	*2 feet (60 cm)*	*Malts well; can grow well in most conditions*
Harrington	*90 days*	*Two-row*	*2 feet (60 cm)*	*Productive; does not thresh well by hand*
Easy thresh hulless	*90 days*	*Two-row*	*3 feet (90 cm)*	*Large head; productive; some lodging; hand threshed*
CDC stratus	*90 days*	*Two-row*	*1.5 feet (45 cm)*	*Large, plump kernels; productive; high yield; drought and disease resistance; low lodging; hand thresh*

Soil Preparation

The soil you choose to plant barley in should be very dry. The barley grown to make malt out of should contain high levels of lime (calcium), phosphorus, and potassium, each of which the plants absorb from the soil.

The best kind of soil for growing barley is **alkaline**. Alkaline refers to a substance that is higher on a **pH** scale. The pH scale refers to how alkaline or acidic a material is. Examples of an acidic substance are orange juice or vinegar; both of these contain mild acids. Examples of an alkaline material are detergents and soaps. Barley is sensitive to any pH below 6.0; thus, a pH between 7.0

14

13 — Bleach

12 — Soapy Water

11 — Ammonia Soluti

10 — Milk of Magnesi‹

9 — Baking Soda

8 — Sea Water

7 — Distilled Water

6 — Urine

5 — Black Coffee

4 — Tomato Juice

3 — Orange Juice

2 — Lemon Juice

1 — Gastric Acid

0

and 8.0 is optimum. If you need your soil pH-tested, contact your local cooperative extension office for recommendations, or you can buy a simple-to-use pH-testing kit at a garden supply store. Different plants require a different level of pH in order to grow. In between the two extremes of alkaline and acidic are neutral substances, such as distilled water. If the soil does not contain the right minerals in it, the soil can be too acidic to grow barley. This will stop the proper growth of barley plants.

If you need to, add some lime (calcium) or some other alkaline material like composted manure to your soil to make it more tolerable for your barley. You can buy these minerals at most garden supply stores and add them to the soil by dumping them on your garden patch evenly over the soil. You can then use a gas-powered tiller, a hand hoe, or shovel to mix the soil.

You should also be careful of excessive nitrogen in the soil, as this will encourage foliage — green leaf — growth rather than sending the energy and nutrients of the plant to the grains. It will reduce the overall yield of your barley. You can also add composted manure, rock phosphate greensand, wood ash, or granite dust to your soil. These nutrients will help increase your yield and grow healthy plants, and they can all be found at a garden supply store locally or online.

Before planting your seeds, you will want to make sure that your garden plot is clear of grass, weeds, and debris. Most of the weed pulling and clearing of debris can be done by hand, but you may need to use a gas-powered tiller to loosen the soil enough to pull out and dispose grass clumps. Use the tiller by going over the soil thoroughly as the tines or blades cut through the soil and dirt.

Remove the grass and make sure the area only contains soil. You can then add any necessary nutrients and mix the soil. Finally, use a garden rake to smooth out the soil in preparation for adding seed.

The best place to grow barley is under full sunlight. However, some shade will not hurt your crop, so it is all right to grow barley with other taller adjunct grains, such as amaranth. When you are picking a plot, try to make it a block shape (a box shape with even sides), because this is the best way for grains to grow. It helps block out any weed growth by not leaving any space for them to grow. The box shape promotes even growing with no space for weeds to grow between the plants. You can also plant them in standard or wide rows, but the block formation does the best to keep weeds at bay. These rows are rectangular-shaped with the plants in a single file formation. There is a space left between the rows in which to walk and maintain the plants.

A 40- by 60-foot (6- by 12-meter) plot will yield about 1 *bushel* of barley. It will take about 2 ¾ pounds of barley seed to cover the plot and produce the bushel. A bushel of barley weighs about 47 pounds (21 killograms) and would fit into a large-sized laundry basket. This is enough barley to make about five batches of all-grain beer, or about 30 batches of extract or partial-mash beer.

Seeds

You can reference a number of resources to buy your seeds. *See Appendix B for a list of resources for purchasing your supplies.* Barley seeds are often bought by the pound and are sold in bags. There are approximately 14,000 barely seeds per pound. Be certain that

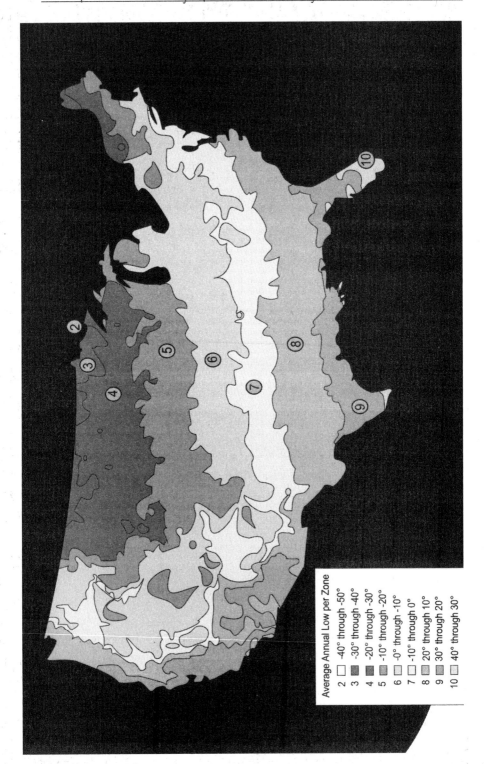

Average Annual Low per Zone

2 -40° through -50°
3 -30° through -40°
4 -20° through -30°
5 -10° through -20°
6 -0° through -10°
7 -10° through 0°
8 20° through 10°
9 30° through 20°
10 40° through 30°

you have seeds ready to be planted in the early spring, as it is a cool-season crop. Cool-season plants are those that grow in areas with winter precipitation and summer drought conditions; barley will grow in the spring and go dormant during the hot and dry months, then begin to grow again when it gets cool. Although barley can grow almost anywhere, it grows the best in cooler climates. Consult the following chart to determine what climate zone you are located in.

If you live in zone 7 or warmer, you will need to sow your seeds in the fall and allow them to stay in the ground over the winter. They will then be ready to harvest in the early summer.

If you need to sow your seeds in the fall, try to do it at least three to four weeks before the first frost, which will allow the seeds to grow a little before winter. Once the temperature and moisture are at the right levels, grains will begin to sprout. On the top of the grain, where it comes to a point, you will see a green shoot begin to emerge.

If you decide to use a block formation, make sure that the blocks are 14 inches wide and allow enough space between blocks for cultivation. You can sprinkle the seed over the plot by hand or with a hand-crank seeder.

Once you have spread the seed, you need a rake to scratch the seed into the ground. Do not cover the seed with too much dirt — use less than an inch. Once the seedlings begin to grow, you will thin them out so that they are about 5 inches apart. You thin them out by choosing a seedling — any seedling — and begin pulling out and discarding any seedlings that are less than 5 inches away.

Then choose another seedling that was the same 5 inches from the first. Continue this until you have seedlings that are at least 5 inches apart from one another. Spacing the seedlings allows them to grow without crowding. If they are too close to one another they will compete for water, minerals in the soil, and more important, sunlight. You will end up with plants that might have stunted growth, may die, or may have a reduced yield.

If you plan to plant the seeds in the spring, you should plan to do it around late March, as you can start growing your barley grains indoors. This is a great idea for small-scale barley growing in your garden. Most of the varieties of barley mentioned in the table are cultivated for malting, and this means that they were bred to sprout well. You can begin indoor planting in seed trays or six-pack cell blocks. These can be purchased in early spring in most stores that sell gardening supplies. The trays contain peat, an organic growing compound. When you add water to the peat, it will swell, and this is because peat is great at absorbing and maintaining moisture. Once you add the water, sprinkle the seeds on top and water them. For a 100-square-foot area, you will plant between 500 and 600 plants.

The trays come with a plastic lid that you need to place over the top to maintain the moisture level. Do not allow the seed tray to dry out. You can add a bit of water occasionally to keep it moist, but it should not contain standing water.

When the seedlings reach an inch (2.5 centimeters) long, it is time to transplant into the ground. This should occur about a week after the sprouts emerge from the grains. Be careful of the delicate roots when you transplant the seedlings. When placing them into the ground, you will want to space them 5 inches apart from one another in each direction.

The good news is that barley is relatively maintenance-free. You just need to be sure to water it during dry periods and make sure that it is well weeded. When watering, you want to just wet the ground, not saturate it. You can water every other day, or when the ground is dry and hard. You may need to get on your hands and knees and literally pull the weeds out of the ground. However, if you planted your barley in a block formation, there will not be many weeds in the garden plot itself, but there may be some growing around the perimeter of it. These weeds will still need to be pulled, but you can use a gas tiller or a hoe to help you. When the grains are about 85 percent golden in color, stop watering them. This will help them dry a bit before harvesting.

Frost can kill young seedlings, or cause them to go dormant. If you need to know your area's frost times, you can ask local farmers, your cooperative extension office, or purchase a copy of *The Old Farmer's Almanac* (**www.almanac.com**). A new edition of the almanac is published every year, and it generally gives good estimates for planting and frost based upon weather patterns and climate. It is not an exact science, but it is usually quite accurate. You can also ask fellow gardeners when other local farmers are planting, as they have the experience to plant at the right time.

Bugs and Disease

There are particular pests and diseases that can damage and even kill your barley. These are the most common pests that affect barley, and these same pests can hurt some of the other plants in your garden as well, especially if you have planted other types of grains like wheat or rye.

Hessian fly

There is one main bug that you should be concerned about with barley, and that is the Hessian fly. This tiny, long-legged fly can be mistaken for a small mosquito. These pests lay eggs in the veins of barley leaves, and when the larvae emerge, they eat the leaves and stop proper water and nutrients from making their way through the plant. If this pest is common in your area, consider planting resistant varieties. You may have to shop around to find the pest-resistant varieties, but they usually cost about the same as other varieties. You can use common pesticides such as Sevin® dust to keep bugs under control. Wear gloves and a face mask when dusting your plants, which is done by hand. You should follow the directions for application on the label of the product.

Aphids

Aphids can also be a problem for barley, especially if there is no wheat or sorghum around, because they prefer these plants to barley. Aphids are small bugs that are often green and are about the size of  a pinhead. They can be easily seen because they usually attack plants in large numbers. Aphids not only can damage the plant by eating it, but they also carry viruses such as yellow dwarf virus. The good news is that there are many natural predators to aphids:

- ladybugs
- hoverfly larvae
- parasitic wasps
- aphid midge larvae
- aphid lions
- crab spiders
- lacewings

The best way to encourage these natural predators is to not use many synthetic pesticides in your garden, as these poisons will also kill beneficial insects. You can hang up ladybug houses that contain a chemical called a ladybug lure to encourage them to live in your garden. *You can buy live lacewings and ladybugs from online sources mentioned in Appendix B.*

Here are some other methods of controlling aphids in your garden:

Inspect your garden daily if possible. If you can catch pests early, you will have a better chance of keeping them under control. It only takes one aphid "colonizer" to produce more than 75 offspring in a week. One colonizer can do this a number of times in its lifecycle. A **colonizer** is just a single aphid capable of laying eggs. You need to look for a small bug or eggs on your plant. You need to be sure to look at the underside of leaves and carefully inspect any new plants you buy at the store. *We will talk about what to do if you find any aphids later in Chapter 5.*

Be sure not to over-fertilize your plants. Aphids are attracted to the new shoots and leaves that are found on over-fertilized plants and herbs. You can avoid this by using "slow release" fertilizers that dissolve in the soil over time rather than all at once.

If you see aphids on your plants, you can use the power of water to get them off. Use a hose with a nozzle that will create a strong spray to spray off the aphids. Once dislodged, aphids will not be able to make their way back to your plant. You also can use a special nozzle called a "Bug Blaster." It creates the powerful water stream that will not only work on aphids, but also on other pests, such as spider mites, mealy worms, and spider mites. *You can find more information about the Bug Blaster in Appendix B.*

If you find that you have an aphid problem, you can use natural solutions that will not harm beneficial bugs, such as spiders and praying mantises, in your garden. You can kill aphids by mixing 2 teaspoons of mild dish soap or even laundry detergent in a 20-ounce soda bottle filled with lukewarm water. Use the solution to wash the leaves, as the soap will wash off the aphid's waxy outer coat and, therefore, cause dehydration and death. You can spray the leaves with the solution in an old spray bottle.

Another mixture you can make to spray on aphids consists of three parts water to one part vegetable oil or horticulture oil, along with a few drops of dish detergent. You can buy horticulture oil at specialty garden supply stores. This solution stops the aphids from breathing through their shell. You should use these sprays at least once a week when you find aphids; continue spraying until they are gone. Make sure that you rinse your plants well before harvesting them.

One other natural way to deal with aphids is remove them from the plant manually. You can do this by cutting off the part of the plant where your see plenty of aphids and get rid of it, away from your garden. This is not a cure to an aphid infestation, but it will slow their progress and can be combined with other methods already described.

A more aggressive way to deal with aphids is using aphid insecticide and aphid spray that can be purchased at a garden supply store. Some of the common products you can buy are insecticidal soaps, oils, and pyrethrins. **Pyrethrins** are produced from an extract of the chrysanthemum flower, and there are synthetic forms called **pyrethroids**. There are also insect growth regulators, or IGRs. These work by mimicking hormones that occur in the aphid's juvenile stage and prevent them from reaching the sexual stage in which they can reproduce. Some IGRs work by interfering with the aphid's ability to molt and, therefore, they cannot grow and mature. **Molting** is the process an insect undergoes in which it sheds its outer exoskeleton in order to grow larger and advance to another stage of development. Some brand names of IGRs are Preclude, Neemix, Enstar 2 Meemasad, and Azatin. These are very strong insecticides, so precautions of masks and gloves should be observed.

Some brands of soaps that are effective on aphids are Safer Insecticidal Soap, Bon-neem Insecticidal Soap, Bonide, Schultz, and Pyola.

Barley cultivars and the types of diseases they are susceptible to

Barley cultivar	Barley yellow dwarf	Barley net blotch	Barley scald	Barley stripe rust	Powdery mildew
Wysor	MDR	MDR	MDR-MDS	MDR-MDS	MDR
Sussex	MDR	MDR	MDR-MDS	LDS	MDR
Starling	MDR	MDS	MDR-MDS	MDR-MDS	MDR
Pennco	MDR	MDS	MDS	MDR	MDR
Pumunkey	MDR	MDS	MDS	MDS	MDR
Nomini	MDR	MDR	MDR	MDS	MDR
Callao	MDR	MDR	MDR	MDS	MDR
Boone	MDS	MDR	LDS	LDS	LDS
Barsoy	LDS	DR	LDS	HDS	LDS

MDS= Medium Disease Susceptibility

MDR= Medium Disease Resistance

LDS= Low Disease Susceptibility

DR= Disease-Resistant

Fusarium head blight

Aside from these pests, a few different plant diseases can affect your barley. The first is called the **Fusarium head blight**, or **scab**, which is a fungal disease that bleaches out the color in the spikelets of barley. This will decrease the yield of the plant. It is spread by spores and affects plants more in damp weather. You can control the damage of this blight by proper crop rotation — change the crop in the same spot year after year. You can see the blight on any part or all of the head as it may appear bleached or the green color has turned white. If the blight infects the stem of the barley, it will cause a brown/purplish discoloration of the stem tissue. You can also find pink-to-salmon-orange spore masses of the Fusarium head blight on infected spikelets after a long period of wet weather. Fusarium head blight can affect wheat as well.

However, there are Fusarium head blight-resistant cultivars. The resistance works by reducing the number of initial infections or reducing the spread of the infection in the plant. If Fusarium head blight is a problem in your area, call your local agricultural extension office to ask what is the best resistant cultivar to plant in your location.

If you have the room to do it, crop rotation can help with the spread of Fusarium head blight. In order to do crop rotation, you must have garden space that is equal in size to the space you are using to grow your barley, because every year you will have to switch from one plot to another to produce the same amount of grain. You can use a smaller plot, but you will produce different amounts of grain every other year. Crop rotation means that you would plant a different type of plant — say, hops — that is not susceptible to the blight the next year in the place where you had planted the barley the year before. In addition, you can try stagger planting your crop. This means that instead of planting all of your grain on the same day, you wait a week between planting blocks or rows. This helps reduce the risk of losing your whole crop, because only some of it may be negatively affected during a period that is favorable for Fusarium head blight infection.

If these simple methods fail to stop Fusarium head blight, you may have to use fungicides. These need to be applied when the head of barley — the part where the seeds are visible — begins to form. The best type of fungicide to use is a triazole fungicide, like Liquid Systematic Fungicide, which you can purchase from a garden supply store. You will need a sprayer that you can also buy at most garden supply stores. This has a reservoir for the fungicide and a hand pump with a hose and nozzle at the top.

When applying the fungicide, spray at a 30-degree angle from the horizontal toward the grain head.

Fungicides used to treat Fusarium head blight

Fungicide	Common product name	Effectiveness
Metconazole	Caramba	Good to very good
Propiconazole	Tilt, PropiMax	Poor
Prothioconazole	Proline	Good to very good
Prothioconazole + Tebuconazole	Prosaro	Very good
Tebuconazole	Folicur, Orius, Monsoon, Embrace, Emboss, TebuStar, Tergol	Fair

Very Good — 85 percent effective or higher
Good — 50 percent to 85 percent effective
Fair — 30 percent to 50 percent effective
Poor — less than 30 percent effective

Barley yellow dwarf

Another area of concern is **barley yellow dwarf**, which is a virus that barley can contract from aphids. This disease will stunt the growth of the barley, yellow its foliage, and decrease the potential yield. This infection is usually localized by the flying patterns of aphids. This disease can be avoided by planting the barley as late in the season as possible. This avoids damage that can occur in the early spring to young foliage. This type of damage can be the most harmful to barley.

Usually the signs of barley yellow dwarf are accompanied by the presence of aphids. The barley plants that are affected are yellowed, and their growth is stunted compared to other plants growing around them. The leaves will have patches of yellow, red, or purple that will extend from the tip of the leaf to the stem. This disease usually occurs in cool weather (from 50 degrees to 68 degrees Fahrenheit) and during moist seasons.

One of the ways to prevent barley yellow dwarf is to plant in the fall after the populations of aphids begin to decline. Try to wait as long as possible for fall planting. Like other diseases and pests, there are cultivars that are resistant or tolerant. The virus does not affect tolerant cultivars as severely if they should contract it. If you are diligent about weeding, this can also help keep yellow barley dwarf at bay, especially if you are sure that you are controlling the grassy weeds. This minimizes the virus and its spread.

Because barley yellow dwarf is a virus, fungicides will have no effect on it. You can treat the seeds before planting to control aphids by applying imidacloprid (Gaucho and other products) or thiamethoxam (Cruiser). This may not always be successful because of the sporadic occurrence of aphid infestations. You can use the methods mentioned earlier to kill off aphid infestations and therefore control the spread of the virus.

Barley stripe rust

The third kind of affliction that commonly affects barley is called **barley stripe rust**. When this disease affects barley, yellow stripes with dots of orange **pustules** on the leaves of the plant appear. Pustules are raised bumps, almost like acne, on the surface of the plant. As it progresses, the pustules become long strips that run parallel to the leaf veins. In an occurrence of a black spore phase, linear black pustules will cover the entire outside of the leaves. This disease comes from a fungus that lives in cool, damp weather. Avoid this fungus by planting as late in the fall or as early in the spring as you can. If your plants seem to be susceptible to this type of disease, you can also elect to purchase resistant varieties.

This disease will overwinter on barley or even wild barley such as foxtail barley, wheat, or other types of grass species. **Overwintering** means that the virus will lie dormant over the winter months and become active when the weather begins to warm again. This disease will begin small, and though it may be hard to detect in large fields of barley, it can be more easily detected in a smaller garden. This disease is more prominent in the Pacific Northwest due to the cool, wet weather that the disease flourishes in.

The best way to combat this disease is to grow disease-resistant cultivars. If you are not growing a disease-resistant cultivar, you can use the fungicides mentioned for use with Fusarium head blight.

Net blotch

Net blotch is a serious disease that can cause loss of yield. It is usually found in western Canada, but it has affected areas of the Midwest, too.

Net blotch will overwinter on barley seeds or crop residue. **Residue** is plant material left over after harvest. The infection is in the form of spores that are spread by rain and wind. These spores are produced on infected plants; the infection will often start during the cool humid weather of spring (50 to 60 degrees Fahrenheit). Spores are produced when the humidity is high and the temperature is warm.

When inspecting your barley, you should look for light brown spots with dark brown, net-like patterns on the leaves, **glumes,** and sheaths. The glumes are the bottom of the bristly parts of the barley plant. The **sheath** is the leaf that grows right under the head of the barley and covers it. On corn, these are the outside leaves you have to peel away.

Eventually, these spots will join together as they become larger and turn into dark brown stripes. Sometimes the infection will appear as dark brown spots with yellow around them. This fungus will destroy leaves and, therefore, reduce the grain yield, because it reduces the carbohydrate content of the barley kernels.

The way to combat net blotch is to use resistant cultivars. You can prevent the spread from year to year by burying any crop residue. Be sure that if you add nitrogen or phosphorus to the soil, adjust the pH so that you do not use too much nitrogen, because this will be more favorable for net blotch outbreaks. As mentioned with Fusarium head blight, you should use crop rotation if possible, with a two-year break between planting barley twice in the same plot. If you cannot use a crop rotation, you can use susceptible barley cultivars one year and a resistant form the next. Try to use seed that has been treated for diseases to reduce the risk of infection.

If you notice the beginning of blotch, treat it with Tilt 250E/Bumper 418EC (propiconazole) and Headline EC (pyraclostrobin). *You can buy these chemicals at a gardening supply center or online at one of places mentioned in Appendix B.*

Scald

Scald is one of the least destructive barley diseases and usually does not result in a high loss. This disease affects the sheaths, leaves, glumes, and awns of barley plant. An **awn** is a stiff bristle at the top of the plant.

If your barley is infected, you will see gray-green spots that are oval and water-soaked (wet looking). These spots are between 1 to 1.5 centimeters long. When scald progresses, the centers of the spots will become bleached out and dry and become a light gray, tan, or white color that has a dark brown margin.

The disease will enter a barley seed and survive there until it is planted. The infection will become the most active when the soil temperatures reach 60 degrees Fahrenheit. If the temperatures reach 72 degrees Fahrenheit or higher, the infection will become stunted.

The infection will overwinter in crop debris from a previous year's infected crop. Spores will form and are then transmitted to the leaves of spring grain by wind and rain. These spores will form when the temperatures reach between 50 to 64 degrees Fahrenheit.

The best way to combat scald is make sure that the seeds you buy are treated for diseases, or use resistant cultivars, implement a crop rotation schedule, bury residue from previous year and, if needed, use fungicides such as azoxystrobin, bromuconazole, cyproconazole, epoxiconazole, fluquinconazole, flusilazole, propiconazole, prochloraz, pyraclostrobin, or tebuconazole.

Powdery mildew

Powdery mildew can affect grains and hops as well. It looks like gray patches of fluffy fungus and grows on the lower leaves of a plant, resembling white powder cushions. On the flip side of the affected leaves, the color turns from a pale green to a yellow. This particular type of fungus only affects the outer layer of leaves and can be scraped off. You may also find this fungus on the sheaths and grain heads.

The leaves might look green for a while, but eventually they will lose color and die. You might also see black points on the leaves, because this is the fungus getting ready to spore. This fungus will overwinter in the plant debris. The spores can be carried great distance on the wind as well. This particular infection requires high humidity in the air to grow; however, in order for spores to be produced, it must be much drier, so it does well whether it is wet weather or dry.

The best defense against powdery mildew is to buy seeds that have been treated with Alphaflo or Foliarflo-C. Most seeds that you buy from online sources have been treated for diseases, but it is a good idea to ask before you buy them. They do not cost any more in price if they have been treated. The second defense is to plant resistant barley cultivars.

Harvesting

Depending on the variety of barley, they should mature in about 70 to 90 days if you planted in early spring, or about 60 to 70 days from the time the barley begins to show shoots if you planted in the fall.

You will know that the grain is about ready to harvest when the plant is dry and the color is light tan to golden; the grain should easily separate from the head of the plant. You can test the barley by pushing a fingernail into a kernel. If the dent remains, then it is ready. This is a sign that the grain has passed its milky stage and is ready to be harvested. The grains should be pale yellow and hard, and you will notice that the heads will be bent over.

Alternatively, you can ask your local cooperative extension office for harvesting guidance, or pay attention to when other local barley farmers are harvesting their barley. You can ask at farmers markets or at the cooperative extension office where other barley farmers are. Once you get through the first year, you will more easily learn what to look for and expect.

Because you will have just a small plot of barley, you must harvest it by hand. You can do this by using a scythe, sickle, or even a gas-powered string trimmer that you would use for weed cutting. If you do not have any other implement, you can use garden shears, especially if your garden is small. A hand sickle is the best to use, and you can buy one online at a garden supply store. *See the stores mentioned in Appendix B.* If you have a large plot, you might want to consider a large, European-style scythe (think of the grim reaper's usual tool). These usually cost about $100 at an online or physical garden store and are lighter and much easier to use than a traditional American scythe.

The goal is not to whack the grain like a bunch of weeds. You should make sure that your blade is sharp by using a whetting stone. If you are not confident that you can sharpen the blade, look in the local directory for blade sharpeners and, for just a few dollars, you can get any of your garden tools sharpened — shears, scythe, and mower blades.

A **whetting stone** can be bought at most hardware stores. It is used for sharpening blades and is made from aluminum oxide. It resembles a small, metal block with a side that has a coarse roughness; the other side is finer. It feels a little like sandpaper.

When you buy a stone, you should soak it overnight in light machine oil, which can also be bought at a hardware store. When you are not using the stone, keep it in a sealed container to prevent it from clogging with dust, because that would make it useless. Right before you are ready to use it, lightly oil it with the machine oil again.

If you look closely at the blade of the sickle or scythe, you will notice that the two sides meet at an angle and form the cutting edge of the blade. Although it may seem smooth to the touch, the blade consists of many tiny serrations or teeth that cannot be seen with a naked eye. When the blade becomes dull, it is because these serrations bend or they become splintered. Using a whetting stone removes the bends and splintered metal so that the teeth are aligned and at a uniform angle along the cutting edge. You will first need to use the coarse side of the stone to remove the damaged teeth on the blade.

To begin, put a drop of the machine oil on the stone. Initially, you will want to use firm pressure, but as the blade becomes finer, use less pressure. Grip the blade on the blunt side and rub from side to side on the coarse side of the stone. You will want to work your way from the base of the blade to the tip. Do this at about a 20-degree angle. First, hold the stone with the short side (non-rough side) against the blade. This is a 90-degree angle. Now half that angle by tipping the rough side toward the blade. Half this distance again and you will have your 20-degree angle. You should try to hold the stone at this angle as you sharpen it. Repeat this procedure with the other side of the blade.

Repeat both sides of the blade two times with the rough side. Repeat the procedure two times with the fine side of the stone, using the same motion and 20-degree angle. The blade should be ready to use.

Once your blade is sharpened, you are ready to cut the grain. You want to use short, controlled swings with your blade. If you are using a hand sickle, hold the stalks of grain and cut the stalks with one smooth motion close to the ground. If you are using a larger scythe, use both hands to swing it from right to left if you are right-handed, and the opposite if you are left-handed. Walk forward as you cut as close to the ground as possible. When you finish cutting a row or large section, you may need to sharpen the blade again. You need to maintain its sharpness for it to cut efficiently.

Once you have cut the grain, bundle it into **sheaves**. You make these sheaves by collecting stalks until you have a bundle that is about 6 inches (15 centimeters) in diameter and binding them with twine or cord — or, you can use a few stems and wrap them around the sheath and tie a knot.

Create a pile by placing six to eight sheaves together, with the cut ends against the ground. Push the ends against the ground. This pile is called a **shock**. The heads of the sheaves should be pressed together and slightly woven, which allows them to support one another. The purpose is to allow air to move around the sheaves and dry them out without letting the grain to touch the ground, which would cause them to absorb moisture or even plant diseases.

You can also place cheesecloth over the top of the shock, which prevents birds from eating the grain while allowing air to circulate and dry the grain. Allow these piles to dry completely before you thresh the grain; this will take about a week. If you know there will be rain in the forecast during that week, make sure you cover the shocks with a tarp to keep them dry. This should be done outdoors, because the sun and wind will ensure they dry quicker and more completely.

Threshing the Grain

Once the grain is dry, it is time to **thresh** it, which is the process of removing the grain from the plant. Follow the steps shown here for a description of the process for threshing the grain that you can easily replicate at home.

Step 1

Spread a large, clean drop cloth or plastic sheeting on a flat, hard surface. A **drop cloth** is a large piece of material that is sometimes used to cover furniture and floors when painting walls in a house. It can be cloth or plastic. For this process, a fabric drop cloth might be easier to use. A garage floor or patio will work well for the threshing process.

Step 2

Pick up the barley plants two handfuls at a time and lay them on the cloth.

Step 3

Use a toy plastic bat or broom handle and hit the grain. Another tool that is used for this step is a **flail**. This tool can be made at home; it is composed of a handle that is 3 feet long with a broom-handle-sized piece of wood attached with a leather thong to another 2-foot piece of wood. You can make this using an old broom handle and a saw. You need to attach the thong securely to the end of each piece of wood. You can do this with some nails that are driven through the leather into the wood. The tool looks similar to a pair of martial arts nunchucks.

Use the flail or bat to strike the head of the grain to release the grain. Be careful using a flail, because you might knock yourself in the head when you are swinging it about. You can expect about a cup of grain for every handful of plant. This process can be hard and takes some work and muscle to accomplish, because the grain may not release easily. Do not worry about the grain going everywhere; it will mostly stay on the cloth you have laid out.

There are a couple of alternatives to this method of threshing. One is to use a clean trash can and strike the heads of the grains on the inside of the can, allowing the seeds to fall to the bottom. This works better than using a flail, but you will find that you will have a lot of chaff, or plant material, along with the seeds that will need to be removed during the next step of winnowing.

The other alternative is treading on the grain. You can walk, or tread, on the grain to loosen the seed. You need to wear clean shoes, and you will need to create a **treading box**. This is a shallow, wooden box that you can make or buy from an art supply store. In the bottom of the box, place 1-inch slats a couple inches apart. Secure the slats with nails. You then place the barley in the box and walk on it. The individual grains will drop between the slats.

Step 4

Discard the **straw** that is left. The straw is the parts of stalk and head that are left from the barley after the grain is removed. You can use the leftovers as farm animal food, mulch, or compost.

Step 5

Once you have removed the straw, pick up the corners of the drop cloth, and pour the grain, chaff, and any remaining bits of straw into a bucket. An old fermentation bucket can work well for this. **Chaff** is the outer casing of the grain seed that protects the ripe seed inside.

Winnowing

Winnowing is the process of separating the grains from the bits of straw. Transferring the contents back and forth between the bucket of grain and an empty bucket can accomplish this step. This process works using a current of air to blow out the light pieces of straw. Do this on a day when there is a stiff breeze, or use a fan to create enough airflow. The heavy grain will fall into the bucket, while the lighter straw and plant material will be blown away. You may not clean the grain completely, but this can happen later after you rinse it during the malting process.

Storage

As with every process required in home brewing, you must be patient during this stage. The growing season of all your components do not coincide, so locating a practical place to store your grain is essential. Plan to complete the malting process with the grain when the weather turns cool again.

You can store the grain in tied burlap sacks in an area where the climate will remain cool and dry. One large burlap sack of grain can hold about a bushel of grain. Dryness is a key component, so a damp basement is not ideal for storage. If stored correctly, unmalted grain can last for years. You can move to the malting process at any time after you have stored your grain, and it is dry. You can put rat and mice traps around your stored grain to prevent them from getting into the sacks. A good place to store grain sacks is in the top of a barn or even an attic.

Malting the Grain

The goal of malting the grain is to convert starch into sugar. This process should be done in late fall or winter, and the area in which the malting will take place should be about 50 degrees Fahrenheit (10 degrees Celsius). You want to be able to control the moisture content and temperature of the grain. If the temperature is too warm, the grain will sprout and create a green shoot. Sprouted grain cannot malt properly and is ruined for beer making. Such warm temperatures in a humid area also promote the growth of fungi, mildews, and molds that will ruin your grain. Avoid warmth and humidity at all costs.

Follow this step-by-step process for malting barley at home, including a list of what you will need to complete the malting phase:

- thermometer (a floating thermometer used for brewing will work)
- two 5-gallon fermentation buckets (food-grade plastic)
- one 5-gallon fermentation bucket with holes drilled in the bottom (⅛-inch in diameter)
- one lid for the fermentation bucket with holes
- large, stainless steel or plastic fermentation spoon
- brewing journal (*See Appendix A for details*)
- a food scale

- aquarium pump with tubing and air stone (optional); use a fresh aquarium stone that has not been used in a fish tank.

- a long-handled spoon

Step 1: Cleanse the grains

First, weighing your grain before you begin the malting process can give you a baseline weight, and you can use this weight to determine when the grain is dry again, because water will be added to the grain during the malting process.

Once you have weighed the grain, rinse it. This removes any left-over debris, straw, chaff, or weed seeds before you begin malting the grain. The easiest way to do this is to place the grain in one of the buckets. Make sure there is plenty of space for water; you should ascertain that you can fully submerge the grains. Gently stir the grain and allow it to settle. The grain is heavy and will sink to the bottom, while debris will float to the top. Use the spoon to skim off the debris. Discard the debris in the trash or compost if you like, but do not dump it into the sink, because the leftovers can cause clogs.

Place the bucket with the holes inside the extra 5-gallon bucket. Pour the grain and water into the bucket with the holes, and allow water to drain into the bucket underneath. Return the grains into the original bucket. Refill the bucket with water, and make sure the grains are submerged again.

Step 2: Steeping the grains

Now you will allow the grains to stay in the water for at least 72 hours. Make sure that the grains are covered with about ½ gallon

(2 liters) of water during this period, and that the temperature remains at 50 degrees Fahrenheit (10 degrees Celsius). You will have to change the water after the initial two hours, then every 12 hours after that. Change the water the same way you did in Step 1 by using the bucket with the holes inside the extra bucket.

If you are using the aquarium stone, place it in the bottom of the bucket and allow it to run. This allows the grains to be aerated and, therefore, instead of changing the grains every 12 hours, you will only have to change them every 24 hours. You will need a place to plug in the aquarium air pump. Attach the tube to the nozzle on the air pump and the other end to the nozzle on the end of the air stone. The stone has many tiny holes in it. When the pump sends air to the stone, tiny air bubbles pass through the stone and expose the liquid to oxygen as it floats to the surface.

Once you have steeped the grains for 72 hours, the grains may appear swollen because they will have taken on water and expanded to 150 percent of the grains' original volume.

Step 3: Germination of the grains

Drain the bucket again as you have done in the past two steps, using the bucket with the holes and the spare bucket underneath. This process should be done in an area that is about 50 degrees Fahrenheit (10 degrees Celsius), with the temperature remaining constant. If it is too cold, you can wrap the bucket with a blanket or an electric blanket with temperature controls. The grains should reach to about 59 degrees Fahrenheit to 65 degrees Fahrenheit (12 to 15 degrees Celsius) but should never exceed 68 degrees Fahrenheit (20 degrees Celsius).

It is during this step that an aquarium stone can be most useful, because it gives you greater control over the germination process. If you do have a stone, pour about a gallon of water into the spare bucket and place the aquarium stone into it. Make sure you do not cut off the air when you place the bucket of grain with the holes in the bottom inside it. The grains should then be suspended over the water, and the bubbling aquarium stone will create a continuously humid, aerated state.

The bubbling water will keep the grains from drying out; it removes excess carbon dioxide, which can stunt the germination of the grain, and it prevents the grain from heating up too much.

If you do not use the aquarium stone, the setup is the same, but you will have to turn the grains two to three times a day with a large spoon or paddle. Push the spoon into the grains, lift a portion of them up, turn the spoon over, and allow the grains to fall back into the bucket. Do this a few times until all of the grains have been turned.

It will take about three days for the grains to complete germination. When you cut open a grain, you should see the acrospire beginning to form. The acrospire should be about ⅔ of the length of the grain and should look like a little green shoot coming out of the top of the grain. When it reaches that point, progress to Step 4.

Step 4: Couching the malt

Once the acrospires have reached ⅔ of the length of the grain, you will give the grain a carbon dioxide bath to stop the growth process; this is called **couching**. This process will ensure that you will be sealing the grain off from oxygen; therefore, only carbon dioxide will remain. This allows the enzymes to convert the starch into fermentable sugar. In Step 3, you released the starches by allowing the acrospire to grow; now, it is time to convert that starch.

The couching process is simple. Attach the lid on top of the bucket with holes on it. You will unplug the air pump that is attached to the aquarium stone and turn the grains to prevent heat buildup at least once a day. Make sure that the acrospire is not continuing to grow. If it is, quickly go to Step 5. If not, allow the grain to couch for one to three days.

Step 5: Kilning the malt

In this step, you will dry out the grain again. This can be a tricky process when done at home. The problem is that it is tough to maintain a constant temperature in an oven. You may want to buy an oven thermometer that can be placed inside so you can monitor the actual temperature, which is often not the temperature set on the dial. Some models have an external gauge so that you do not need to open the oven to see the reading. These can be bought at most kitchen stores or hardware stores for about $20. You can also use a commercial food dehydrator to do the job. The problem is that they cannot hold much grain at one time. Using this method is long and tedious, so their usefulness is limited.

The solution to this problem, if you intend to continue kilning your own grains for use in beer making, is creating your own grain dryer. *At the end of this section, you can find directions on how to build one out of an old refrigerator.*

If you intend to create dark malts, a kitchen oven can work sufficiently to dry your grains. You should use the lowest setting on your oven with a cookie sheet to dry the grains. Spread the grains evenly across an ungreased cookie sheet and place into the oven, stirring them with a spoon occasionally as they dry. It takes about 48 hours to dry out 5 pounds (2.3 kilograms) of malt. However, this is not the most energy-conscious way to kiln malt. Below is a process of creating a more energy-efficient way to dry your malt out.

Remember, you weighed your malt at the beginning of this process. You will know your malt is dried when the weight is the same or slightly less than the original weight.

Photo courtesy of USDA Natural Resources Conservation Service.

How to build a malt dryer
out of a refrigerator

You will need to find an old refrigerator or freezer. It does not have to work, but you must be able to close it. Landfills, junkyards, and appliance stores are a great place to look. Make sure that you keep this dryer somewhere safe — you might want to attach a lock to prevent any children from going inside it. Older-model refrigerators lock from the outside, making them dangerous for animals or children who could get stuck inside. Newer models usually open and close easily with a magnetic closing device.

If you need to dispose of the Freon™, do so safely. Freon is not actually a gas; it is a product name that refers to any number of refrigerants called "chlorofluorocarbons." Direct exposure to Freon can be dangerous to people with a history of heart problems, because inhaling the gas can cause irregular heartbeats and palpitations, which is the feeling of your heart pounding in your chest.

The most serious side effect of Freon exposure would occur at the time of initial exposure. People who have a history of heart problems should be especially concerned about Freon because it can cause cardiac arrhythmia (irregular heartbeat) and palpitations at high concentrations. Small amounts of Freon from leaking appliances should not pose any significant health risk, even for someone with heart problems. It dissipates quickly and does not have any long-term effects. Still, you should be careful and not try to deal with it yourself, because it is illegal to dispose of Freon without permission. It is best left to the experts.

The diagram below shows a picture of how to construct the dryer. Follow these steps:

1. Create a vent on the old unit in the top and the bottom.

2. Create drying trays from a nylon window screen over a frame. You can buy the material at a hardware store, or you may have old screens that can be cleaned and used.

3. Add a hot plate on a shelf just above the bottom of the refrigerator. A hot plate looks like a burner from the top of a stove that you can plug into the wall and has a heating dial on the side. There should be enough room underneath for a small fan. Make sure it is not touching anything that can burn. Place the fan at the bottom and tilt it so the air is blowing upwards. This will dry out the sprouted grain. The dried, sprouted grain allows you to create pale base malt.

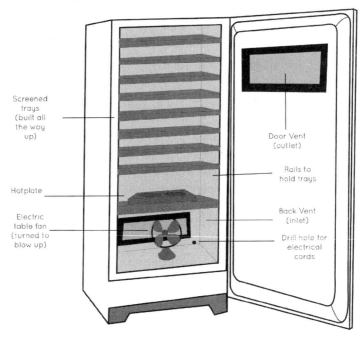

Once you have the dryer constructed, take the couched grain and place it on the screens. Turn on the fan and hot plate and seal the door. It can still take about 48 hours to fully dry — weigh your grains to make sure. Your grain should weigh the same amount, or slightly less, than they did when you first thrashed them from the stalks. These dried and finished grains are then ready to use.

Tip: If you are unsure whether your grains have converted and are fully malted, try this trick: Fill a bucket with water. Take a small handful of grain and toss it into the water. Grains that have not converted will sink to the bottom of the bucket; grains that are under-modified will float like fishing buoys — vertical. Fully modified grains will float like boats — horizontal.

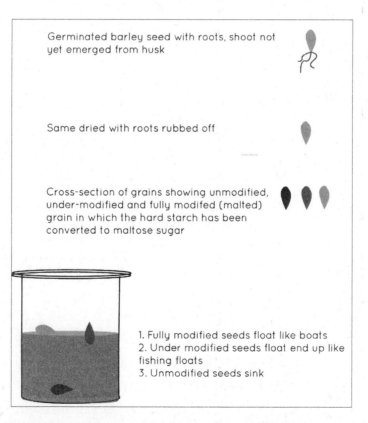

Germinated barley seed with roots, shoot not yet emerged from husk

Same dried with roots rubbed off

Cross-section of grains showing unmodified, under-modified and fully modifed (malted) grain in which the hard starch has been converted to maltose sugar

1. Fully modified seeds float like boats
2. Under modified seeds float end up like fishing floats
3. Unmodified seeds sink

Step 6: Roasting the grains

Once you are sure the grains are dried, it is time to roast the grains. You will be able to produce roasted grains using your kitchen oven. Make sure that you spread the grains no thicker than ¾-inch (2 centimeters) deep on a baking sheet. Once you have roasted your grains, allow them to cool before storing them. They should then be stored for a week before they are used for brewing.

Common malts and how to create them

Type of malt	How to create it
Toasted malt	Roast malt at 350° F (178° C) for 10 to 15 minutes. The result will be malt that is golden and smells toasty.
Munich malt	Roast malt at 350° F (178° C) for 20 minutes. The result will be slightly toasted malt.
Vienna malt	Roast between 215° F and 225° F (102° to 107° C) for at least three hours.
Roasted barley	This is unmalted barley. It should be clean and dry. You will roast it at 400° F (200° C) for 70 minutes until it is a deep, golden brown.
Black Patent malt	This malt should be thinly spread on a sheet. Roast it at 350° F (178° C) for 80 minutes. You need to watch this closely and stir often to prevent it from burning. Open the windows — this malt will smoke as it is roasting.

Caramelize the Grains

Caramelization is the temperature at which a sugar will break down. This is important when preparing grains for the wort — different levels of caramelization will impart different colors and tastes to the beer. As you can see in the table, different sugars will caramelize at different temperatures. One factor that must be present in order for caramelization to occur is low moisture content in the grain.

Type of sugar	Temperature required to caramelize
Sucrose	*320° F (160°C)*
Glucose	*320° F (160°C)*
Galactose	*320° F (160°C)*
Maltose	*356° F (180°C)*

Caramelized malts

These malts are kilned at high temperatures when they are still moist, rather than completely dried out. The sugars are converted to fermentable sugars, and the high heat caramelizes them. This turns the ingredients into a liquid-like sugar that hardens when it cools. This process gives a beer a sweet, malty flavor and contributes to smoothness when drinking it. *See Appendix D for a table of the different kinds of caramel malts.*

Caramelizing grain can be a little tricky for a home brewer. You have to get the grains to a specific temperature and hold that temperature until the grains caramelize. This depends on the type of malt you want to create. It is essential to use green malt that has not been kilned. You will place the grain instead into a damp or wet oven; the grain will use this water to undergo mashing. The essential process converts the sugar in the grains into fermentable sugars.

In all grain brewing, when the grains are mashed, the resulting liquid is called the malt, which is used for creating beer. In this case, the grains have been kilned, malted, and crushed so that when the sugars are converted, they are taken away from the grain and create the wort for brewing. In the case of caramelization, the malt is not kilned and is not crushed; therefore, when the sugars convert, they remain in the hull. When the starches are converted into sugar in the hull, the temperature is lowered, allowing the sugar to crystallize. The resulting grain is then dried with heat; the temperature at which the drying takes place will determine the flavor and color of the final beer.

Making your own crystal/caramel malts at home

As with any roasted or kilning of grains at home, creating caramel malts can be a little tricky, but it is quite possible. The important factors are time and temperature.

Step 1

You will need to hydrate the green grain you want to use for 24 hours. You do this by soaking the grains in water. Add the grains to a fermentation bucket and pour in water until it covers the top of the grains. Make sure that the water does not have chlorine in it. You can usually buy gallons of spring water from a grocery store for less than $1 per gallon, or you can use a water filter you attach to your sink or pour through into a water pitcher.

Step 2

Drain the grains and put the wet grains in the oven at 160 to 165 degrees Fahrenheit for at least three hours. You can pour the grains through a colander, so that it catches the grains and allows the water to pass through. You can place the grains in a casserole dish; however, you want to make sure that the grain bed is about 2 inches deep. You want the starch to turn to sugar, which this step allows. If you do not convert the starch to sugar, you will be left without any sugars to caramelize. Make sure you are testing the temperature of the grain bed. It should be about 155 to 165 degrees Fahrenheit. Make sure it does not get too hot, or it will destroy the enzymes needed for the starch conversion.

Step 3

You will need to brown and caramelize the malt. The longer it browns, the darker and more caramel-flavored the malt will become. These darker grains can be used to make stouts and brown ales. In order to do this, take the grains that have been converted and put them in two casserole pans. The grain bed should be about 1-inch deep.

Step 4

Preheat your oven to 220 degrees Fahrenheit. Place the grains in the oven and stir them with a long-handled spoon every 30 minutes until the grains are dry and crisp. Within two hours, they should begin to darken. If you stop here, your caramel grains should be between 15 degrees Lovibond and 20 degrees Lovibond.

Step 5

If you want to continue the process for a darker grain, you should spray the grains with water and moisten them slightly. This way, your grains will continue to mash rather than just roast. You will need to raise the temperature in the oven to 300 degrees Fahrenheit. Your grains should continue to darken through different stages of Lovibond. Watch your grains closely and stop when you have created the type of grain you wish to use to create a specific type of beer. You can use the Lovibond scale on the back cover of this book to help you determine what degree of roasting you require.

Step 6

When your grains reach about 19 degrees Lovibond, raise the temperature to 350 degrees Fahrenheit. Watch your grains constantly and stir them every 15 minutes. Be careful, though; your grains will be darker than you think when they are in the oven, so take them out before they reach the level you think they should be (a lighter color than you think it is).

Store your grains in a dry, cool place, like a closet or in a cabinet, until you are ready to add them to the wort during the brewing process.

Chapter 3

Working With Other Grains

*"A fine beer may be judged with only one sip, but it's
better to be thoroughly sure."*
— **Czech proverb**

*I*n Chapter 2, you learned how to work with barley and the process *of converting the starch in the barley into fermentable sugars.* But, you can grow and use more plants in beer than just grain. This chapter will explore some of these unusual beer adjuncts to help broaden your home brewing and gardening horizons.

Amaranth

This grain was used by the ancient civilizations of Mesoamerica: the Inca, Maya, and Aztecs. It is not used as much these days as a traditional grain because it has been replaced with corn as the grain of choice, but for a home brewer, it can create a nutty-flavored beer. The seeds can be bought at gardening stores, because the plant is sometimes used in landscaping. *Many of the resources in Appendix B sell amaranth seeds.* The great thing is that amaranth is a hardy plant to grow. It usually self-seeds year after year and grows with little or no cultivation. It is a productive grain that is

AMARANTH

as pretty to grow, as it is tasty in beer, with long, colorful heads of purple and red.

Amaranth can be grown alongside barley, because they grow in similar soil and climate and will not compete for sunlight or nutrients in the soil. Both can grow anywhere from 4 to 10 feet (1.2 to 3 meters) tall. These are huge plants that have a large seed head that can be different colors, depending upon the variety.

Amaranth varieties

Name	Maturity	Height	Description
Opopeo	*100 days*	*7 feet (2.1 m)*	*Can grow well in cold areas; early season variety; maroon seed heads*
Burgundy	*90-120 days*	*5-8 feet (1.5-2.4 m)*	*Productive; small, white seeds; red foliage; red seed heads*
Golden	*90-95 days*	*6-9 feet (1.8-2.7 m)*	*Very productive; white seeds; gold seed heads*
Golden giant	*98-120 days*	*6-7 feet (1.8-2.1 m)*	*Very productive; mid-season variety; up to 1 pound (.45 kg) of seeds per plant; bronze-stripped leaves; orange-gold seed heads*

Planting amaranth

The soil preparation will be similar to what you did for barley. You will need to clear the area of any weeds, and you can benefit from using a gas tiller to turn the soil; you also can do this by hand with a shovel.

It will take about 2 pounds of seeds to plant an acre plot of amaranth, which will produce up to 4 pounds of seed for use in beer making, which can be used in about eight 5-gallon batches of beer. The seeds can be bought from many different online sources. There are about 1,050 seeds per gram. You can buy seeds by the gram, ounce, or even pound.

Begin planting seeds after the last frost and after the soil has begun to warm some. This occurs after about three or four sunny days that take the chill out of air and the soil feels warm to the touch. The best months are late May or early June. Fortunately, amaranth can grow in almost any soil condition, but for the best results, it should be planted in well-drained soil. The optimum pH conditions are between 6.0 and 7.5.

You must pick a place that has full sun. When you are ready to plant, dig **furrows** ⅛- to ¼-inch deep (3 to 6 millimeters). A furrow is a small trench that is dug in the earth by a plow or hoe. Sow the seeds thickly into these furrows/rows, which should be spaced about 18 inches (45 centimeters) apart.

Make sure that you continue to water the ground daily until you see the first leaf appear, then stop. You will not need to water the sprouts further unless there is a severe drought condition. Only fertilize with plant fertilizer once while they are growing, because using too much will cause them to grow too high and lodging will occur.

When the seedlings appear, you should thin them to 10 to 18 inches (25 to 45 centimeters) apart. The seedlings will be small, green spouts making their way upwards through the soil. The thinning process is the same as the one used with barley. Start with a seedling on the end of a row and measure 10 to 18 inches. All of the seedlings between the first seedlings and the one closest to your measured length should be pulled from the ground and discarded.

Harvesting amaranth

You will begin to see large seed heads grow on the grain by mid to late summer. The seed heads look like long feather dusters. By early autumn, they will mature and be ready to harvest. You will know they are ready to harvest if the seeds fall out of the seed head when disturbed.

If you live in a dry area, with low humidity, you can allow the plants to dry on their own. You can check the humidity level of your region by looking at **www.weather.com** and checking average humidity levels for your area. If you do not live in a dry area, you should cut off the seed heads and allow them to dry completely before threshing.

The good news is that you can harvest and thresh the amaranth right from the plant. Hold the head over a bucket and rub the seeds right off the plant with your other hand. If they are ripe, they will easily fall into the bucket. Allow them to dry in a cool, dry place, then winnow the grain the same way you did with barley.

Malting amaranth

The process of malting amaranth is similar to malting barley and is relatively easy to do.

Step 1

Place the grain in a large jar, fill it with enough room-temperature water to cover the grain, and cover with cheesecloth for 12 hours. After this time, you will want to rinse the grain with cold water and drain. Place the jar containing the grain in a warm, dark place. Continue to rinse the grain at least three times a day.

Step 2

Allow grain to sit for three to four days in the jar. Keep an eye on the grain, and look to see if the acrospires have formed. You will see a white circle around the top of the grain when this occurs. You will notice that the center of the seed has darkened, and there may be some root beginning to grow from the seed. Once this has occurred, proceed to Step 3.

Step 3

In this step, you will kiln the grain to dry it out. Evenly place the amaranth seed on a cookie sheet or any other shallow pan. Set the oven on its lowest setting for two to six hours. If you have a gas oven, just leave on the pilot light. For every pound (.45 kilograms) of grain, you will yield about 6 ounces (171 milligrams) of malt for brewing.

Allow the grain to cool and store in a cabinet or closet for a week before using.

Corn

Corn is used as an adjunct of many American lager beers, such as Budweiser, Coors, and Miller. It can add sweetness to beer and, as malt, fermentable sugars. The Indians in the Andean mountains of South American have been making beer for centuries from corn, which they call *chicha de jora*. This frothy beer is not bottled, but rather consumed straight from the fermentation vessel.

There are thousands of corn hybrids to choose from to make your beer; they are just too numerous to list. You should be using corn that is fit for eating, not seed corn. The chart below contains some of the corns the Andeans use to make their historic beer. They are unusual in both color and flavor.

Corn varieties

Name	Maturity	Height	Description
Ashworth	*60-85 days*	*4-5 ½ feet (1.2-1.5 m)*	*Cold-tolerant; open pollinated; 6- to 7-inch (15-18 cm) ears; bright yellow kernels*
Black Aztec	*68-110 days*	*4-6 feet (1.2-1.8 m)*	*White kernels mature to black color; 7-inch (17 cm) ears; makes good chicha de jora beer*
Peruvian morado	*90-110 days*	*4-6 feet (1.2-1.8 m)*	*Dark violet kernels; 2 ½- to 6-inch (6-15 cm) ears*
Bloody butcher	*100-120 days*	*8-12 feet (2.4-3.7 m)*	*Red and pink kernels; two to six ears per stalk*

Planting corn

Corn can be a tricky crop to plant. It is not like other grains, because it needs special conditions and care. You can buy corn seed from many online sources, or from seed and garden stores locally. There are between 110 to 250 seeds per ounce, and you can purchase corn by the ounce or pound. One acre of seed-planted crop can yield 7,110 pounds of corn; this includes the cobs.

You need to find a plot that contains rich, moist **loam** for soil. Loam is a mixture of soil that contains clay, silt, and sand, with a proportion of 20:40:40. You can sow the seeds after the last frost; the soil should be at least 65 degrees Fahrenheit. Plant the seeds three at a time, and space them at least 12 inches (30 centimeters) apart. You should sow the seeds at least 1 inch (2.5 centimeters) deep. You can create blocks of seeds that are 30 inches (76 centimeters) apart. You can also plant corn in rows, but you will need at least four rows, and they must be 24 to 30 inches apart.

After a couple of weeks, and depending on the variety of corn, the seedlings reach 4 inches (10 centimeters) tall; this is the time when you will need to thin them to one plant every foot (30 centimeters). Stick closely to these guidelines because placing the corn plants too close to one another will stunt their growth, and having them too far away from one another will not allow normal **pollination**. Pollination is necessary for sexual reproduction in a plant. It occurs when pollen is transported from one plant to the same type of plant in order to fertilize it. This can happen by the wind, or from pollinators like bees and butterflies. In corn, however, pollination occurs by the wind, rather than by insects. In fact, some varieties can crossbreed through pollination by wind when plants are as much as a ¼ mile apart. You must have at least four rows so that proper pollination can occur with the corn silks. Without this pollination, the kernels will not grow.

Make sure the ground does not get too dry. If it has been longer than a week since the ground was watered or since there was rain, the ground might become too dry. Corn grows the best when it grows steadily. If you allow the plants to get dry, this can interrupt steady growth, stunting the plant. Additionally, you will need to apply between 1 to 2 inches of water to your corn each week. You can do this with a hose with a sprayer nozzle attached, or you can place a small sprinkler in the garden. Those interested in conserving water can use what is called a porous soaker hose. This specially made hose with pinhole openings allows water to soak slowly into the ground, which prevents water being wasted by evaporation. The sprayer, sprinkler, or soaker hose can be bought at most hardware stores or garden supply centers. If you have planted the corn in well-mulched, nutrient-rich soil, you may get away with watering every two weeks, because this type of soil usually holds moisture better.

If you live in a climate where it rains more than once or twice a week, you will not have to worry about watering, even if there are short dry spells. The most important time to ensure there is adequate water is when the ears of corn are beginning to fill out with kernels.

Once your corn is planted and beginning to grow, make sure that you take care of weeding regularly; this will be the biggest job you have. Do a good job of weeding, because even if the weeds are not choking out the corn, the weeds can deplete the soil of necessary nutrients. These roots stabilize the plant and keep it growing upright.

Hoeing

Using a hoe is easier and more effective than just using your hands to pull weeds. A hoe, when used correctly, will kill weed seedlings before you can even see them above ground. Thus, hoeing actually reduces the number of future weeds.

Throughout this book, you will notice that many of the plants are planted in rows with space in between. This allows you the space needed to hoe and remove weeds. When you plant in a straight row, this provides you the space to hoe weeds without damaging plants and makes it easier to recognize plant seedlings from weed seedlings. Planting in a straight row also allows you to hoe by pushing or pulling in a straight line. This is a much easier and efficient way to hoe rather than to try to hoe around plants in sideways or circular motions.

It is best to hoe before your garden is overrun with weeds. If you hoe regularly, you can kill the seedlings before they create deep roots and are harder to remove; plus, killing them early prevents them from reproducing. Thus, you should begin hoeing right after you plant seeds. Make sure you have clearly designated where your rows of plants are so that you do not accidentally dig up seeds or small seedlings.

If given a chance, a weed that is chopped off or dug up with a hoe may try to re-root. This is why you should hoe when the ground is dry, as the weeds stand less of chance of re-rooting. It is also important to remove the weeds with a rake or by hand; after you have hoed, throw them in a garbage bin. Do not put them in a compost pile, or they could potentially root there and spread.

There is a technique to hoeing. You want to stand up as straight as possible when hoeing to take pressure off your back. If you do not, you may find your back is very sore the next day. Make sure that the length of the handle of the hoe is sufficient for your size. If it is too short, it will be difficult not to stoop over; on the other hand, if it is too long, you may not be able to grip it right for the most efficient hoeing. The best way to choose the right length of a hoe is to measure from the bottom of your ear to the ground. This will give you the optimum length of the hoe that is best for you.

When choosing the right hoe, look for one that has a blade at the bottom that is forged as one piece, rather than one where the blade is only riveted to the neck. The riveted types are cheaply made and will not last very long without coming apart. The neck is the swan neck-like part that connects the blade to the handle. Be sure that the hoe's blade is between 4 and 6 inches wide.

While you are using a hoe, you must cut the weeds away from their roots, just below the surface of the soil. You want to be as close as possible because if you dig too high or too low, you might unintentionally allow the weed to live. The best depth for your hoe is about ½ to ¾ inches deep into the soil. If you dig too deep, you may pull the entire weed up which would allow it to re-root, and if you do not cut deep enough, you may allow too much plant to be attached to the root, which will allow it to regenerate and grow. You may push or pull the hoe, but be mindful of the depth as you scratch your way through weeds.

Keep in mind that there is more than one type of hoe. One is called a cutting hoe, and the other is referred to as a draw hoe. The draw hoe is used when planting seeds, as it creates furrows like the ones needed for planting amaranth. This may not be the best for removing weeds. It is called a draw hoe because you use it by pulling it toward you, and it is great for breaking up compacted soil that makes it hard to plant seeds. You can use this type of hoe to plant seeds by holding the hoe at a slight angle, so the corner is pointing into the dirt. You can then pull the hoe and make a small trench to place seeds into.

The second kind of hoe, the cutting hoe, is more suited for weeding. It is sometimes referred to as a push or Dutch hoe. These hoes have a sharper blade than the draw hoe because they are designed specifically for cutting weeds. The hoe is used differently from the draw hoe. Rather than dragging it, the hoe's blade is pushed into the soil about ½ to ¾ inches, and then is pushed back and forth so that the weeds are cut from their roots in the right position.

Another way to deal with weeds instead of weeding all the time is to mulch the area with hay or straw. Plant the seeds as you normally would, and cover with about an inch of mulch. Once the plants have begun to grow and you have thinned them out, add about 3 to 4 more inches of mulch. You can evenly spread the mulch around the plants to cover the ground, allowing enough room for the plant to grow.

Corn requires plenty of nitrogen from the soil to grow and produce a large yield. Before planting, take a soil sample to your local cooperative extension office; they can help you determine how much fertilizer you should add to your soil for planting corn. If this is not an option, then you can use a standard amount of 4.5 pounds of 5:10:5 (nitrogen, phosphorus, and potassium ratio) fertilizer for every 100 square feet of corn.

You should rotate your corn every year, because corn can deplete the soil's nutrients. Try growing your crops like farmers often do and rotate with alfalfa, peas, or beans, which will add nitrogen back into the soil.

Bugs, pests, and diseases

There are a few different bugs you should be concerned about when planting corn. Following is a chart that describes the pest and what to do if you encounter it. You can buy pest and disease resistant corn cultivars. Ask the people you buy from what types of resistant cultivars they offer.

Wireworm

A wireworm is actually the larva form of the click beetle. It is slender and hard bodied. Its coloring can vary from black to tan, and it is about ¼ inch to an inch long. Wireworms feed on germinating seeds, bore into roots, and feed on seedlings, which will stunt the growth of the plant. Wireworms will eat the seed on the bottom of newly planted seedlings. As the corn grows larger, wireworms will attack the stem and bore below ground. The plant will wilt and die.

Wireworms love carrots; so one of the best ways to deal with these pests is to bury carrots every 3 to 5 feet along rows, which will attract the wireworms. This is called **baiting**. Pull up carrots every few days and dispose of bugs, then rebury the carrot. You can also treat your corn with granular pesticides.

Corn borer

The larvae of corn borers can be identified by their pinkish-tan body. They can be found boring into the ears of corn and the leaves. The adult form is a moth-like insect that is small, tan, and flies at night. It is about ½-inch long, and their wings form a **delta shape**, or triangle, when they are resting.

Corn borers damage corn by tunneling into the cornstalk, which weakens it. The boring will disrupt the plant's vascular (water-moving) tissues, which can interfere with the flow of water, sugars, and nutrients. You will notice the damage, because severe lodging can occur and the ears will drop down rather than facing upwards.

Buy resistant varieties of corn. Be sure to mulch the stalks and debris from the corn between years of planting. The area where you are growing corn should be clear so the borers will not overwinter for the next season.

Corn earworms

When corn earworms hatch, they attach themselves to the plant for a feeding site. This is usually near the reproductive part of corn where the ears form. The larva can range from 1.5 to 24.8 millimeters in size. The larva can vary in color from orange, light brown, green, yellow, to black. They usually have narrow, dark bands on the center of their backs. They have light colored heads and have small spikes on their body that make them feel rough to the touch.

When they mature, they will burrow into the ground and go through the pupa stage, which occurs for about two weeks during the summer. They then emerge as moths with forewings that are a yellowish brown.

The larvae do damage to corn by feeding on the corn silks, which interferes with proper pollination. They will also feed on the tips of the ears of corn as well. You can tell that you have this type of pest because they leave behind a sawdust material called frass. The best way to deal with these pests is to apply *Bacillus thuringiensis* and cut off damaged parts of the ear. Make sure you clean up before winter, because moths can lay eggs and overwinter.

Birds, deer, and raccoons

Some more-common larger pests will eat your corn and damage or destroy stalks in the process. Much of this damage is done in the dark of night. One way to discourage these animals is to put two strings over seeds you have sown between stakes on the end of the row. This will prevent birds from eating the seeds. To deal with raccoons, you may have to erect an electric fence, and erect an 8-foot fence to keep deer out. Fences must be at least 3 feet away from the corn to prevent an animal from leaning over and eating it.

In addition to insects and animals, diseases that can destroy corn. Some are bacterial and some fungal. There are many different kinds of resistant corn varieties and some infections are more prominent in certain areas of the U.S. It is best to contact your local agricultural extension office for advice about wxhich resistant varieties they recommend in your area.

Corn smut

Corn smut is one of the common diseases that can affect corn. In Mexico, people actually harvest this fungus — *Ustilago maydis* — for food. It can enter a corn stalk through wounds caused by hoes, insects, or other problems. If you see the smut, which looks like mushroom-like material, forming you should remove and destroy the affected plants. The spores can survive in the soil for years, so it is important not to compost affected stalks.

Corn smut feeds off the corn plant and reduces its yield. It replaces kernels with tumors called galls, which contain blue-black spores that can spread the infection by wind or rain. Most commercial corn producers have to destroy the infected plants to prevent the spread, and this is the best way to combat it. There is very little natural resistance in corn to the disease. The spores will over-winter in corn plant debris and even in the soil, so crop rotation can help the spread. The infection occurs more often when there are warm, dry, early summers, which are followed by a period of heavy rains. If you see the galls beginning to form remove the diseased part of the plant, put it into a paper bag, and burn it to make sure you do not release any live spores.

Fungal infections

Seed rot and seedling blight

When a seed is germinating, fungi in the soil or in the seed can attack it. Some of the species of fungi are *Pythium, Diplodia*, and *Fusarium*. These types of diseases will kill a seedling. These more often occur in soil that is too compacted, wet, or cold. You can purchase some disease-resistant corn cultivars. One way to pre-vent these types of fungus is to make sure you buy seeds that have been treated with a fungicide, like those mentioned for bar-ley.

Southern corn leaf blight

This fungus causes sores or lesions on the leaves of the corn plant. They appear as long, tan sores that are up to an inch in length on the leaves that have brown borders. This fungus can destroy a corn plant. Crop rotation and destroying corn residue after har-vest is the best way to combat it. You can also buy resistant cul-tivars.

Northern corn leaf blight

When this fungus attacks corn, it looks like tan to grayish-green lesions that are elliptical and range from 1 to 6 inches long on the leaves of corn. The infection begins on the lower leaves first and then does the most damage to the upper leaves. This fungus does the most damage in moderately warm and moist weather conditions. The damage caused by this blight can kill corn plants, and it gives a gray look to the leaves. The treatment is similar to that with southern blight: crop rotation, removal of plant debris, and planting resistant cultivars.

Anthracnose

Anthracnose is another fungal disease that appears as small, either oval or elongated, water-soaked spots. These spots can appear at any time on the leaves of corn. As the disease progresses, the spots may grow to ½-inch long, and the color will change to tan at the center, which is surrounded by red, reddish-brown, or yellow-orange borders. These spots will grow together to affect the entire leaf and kill it.

If the infection attacks the stalks of the corn, the long stems that grow from the ground, it will appear as black, linear streaks under the outer layer of the plant. These legions can grow into large, oval, black areas and measure between a ½ to 1 inch. If the infection takes over the stalk, whole black areas will be visible on the stalk. In severe infections, large areas of the stalk may be blackened. When this happens, the upper part of the corn plant will die.

Like other fungi, anthracnose will overwinter on plant debris, and so the way to handle it is crop rotation, destroy plant residue, and plant resistant cultivars.

Southern rust

There are types of fungi that are referred to as rust, because they are a bright orange or golden brown color. Southern rust can be seen as circular to oval pustules and give the leaves that they infect a rusted look. These pustules are pinhead-sized and are full of orange spores that can be rubbed off a leaf. Unfortunately, this means the spores can easily spread by wind and can travel hundreds of miles. This type of plant rust can be found in warm and humid climates. The way to combat it is by planting resistant cultivars. This rust can damage corn and even kill it.

Common rust

Common rust is different, because it can occur in subtropical areas. It looks a bit darker than southern rust and the pustules are longer as well. Common rust will appear as rust clumps on corn leaves. Common rust can survive overwinter in areas where temperatures do not go below freezing. Like southern rust, the best way to combat common rust is to plant resistant corn cultivars.

Gray leaf spot

Gray leaf spot will infect the leaf sheaths and leaf blades. It appears as gray or pale-brown lesions that are long and narrow and run parallel with leaf veins. These lesions are about ¼ inch wide and about 1 inch long. If the disease progresses, these lesions will grow together into long stripes and will kill the leaf, which will affect the yield of the plant. The way to prevent this fungus is crop rotation, destroying plant debris, and planting resistant cultivars. It is also important to use a tiller on the soil as well.

Brown spot

This type of fungus looks like you would expect. Small, purplish-brown to reddish brown spots will appear on the leaf blades, sheaths, and stalks. If the disease progresses, the spots will merge into large brown blotches. This disease will weaken stalks and cause them to lodge and will destroy leaf sheaths. The best way to prevent this disease is to plant resistant cultivars.

Stalk rots

Stalk rot is caused by *Diplodia zeae* and *Fusarium* species of fungi. These infections will destroy a corn plant and occur after a large amount of rainfall in the late growing season. If cold, leaf diseases, or insects injure stalks, they are more susceptible to be attacked by these fungi. When this fungus attacks, it causes the stalk to ripen prematurely and will cause stalks to break and fall. If the corn touches the ground, then the corn is at risk for rotting.

Ear and kernel rots

These types of rots are caused by the same species of fungi that cause stalk rot. These infections occur during harvest time if the weather is warm and the ground is wet. This infection will decrease corn yield, and the seed is useless for beer or as seed because the kernels have been too damaged. A Diplodia rot appears as white to grayish-brown on ears of corn, and a Fusarium will appear as a pink or reddish rot of the ear.

Nematodes

A nematode is a small to microscopic roundworm that can be parasitic to plants. Thousands of different types of nematodes exist and some can be very damaging to a garden. They not only attack and kill plants like corn, but they can also carry other plant diseases and infect the plants as well.

In the case of corn, nematodes exist in the soil and will attack and damage the roots, which stunts the plant's development and impairs its ability to take in water and nutrients. You can recognize affected plants because they will appear small, undernourished, and their growth will be stunted as compared to corn around them. Nematodes will not usually attack plants in a uniform way, so you may find plants all around the garden that are affected rather than a patch of corn. Two common types of nematodes are the stubby root and the sting nematodes.

These are only a couple of the types of nematodes that can affect corn. Every part of the country and world has different types of nematodes in the soil. For many of the cases, a nematicide can be used. A **nematicide** is a type of chemical that is formulated to kill nematodes. The other way to combat them is crop rotation and the destruction of crop debris.

Stubby-root

This type of nematode feeds on the root tips rather than actually entering the roots like other sorts of nematodes. The damage they cause stunts the growth of the roots, hence the name. The result of the stubby roots is that the ears formed on the plant are very small and underdeveloped.

Sting

This type of nematode feeds on the outside of the roots rather than entering them. They also feed on the root tips and along the sides of the roots as well. The roots will become blackened and will appear sunken and dead. Eventually, if untreated, the root will die. If they do not die, the plants will grow only to about 8 inches tall. These types of nematodes are found most often in soil that is made of 80 percent or more of sand. The sting nematodes can work in tandem with stubby root nematodes and cause a huge yield loss.

Corn viruses

A couple of viruses worth mentioning can affect corn. One is the maize dwarf mosaic virus (MDMV) and the other is maize chlorotic dwarf virus (MCDV). These diseases can cause losses of between 5 to 90 percent of a cornfield. Aphids and leafhoppers from infected Johnson grass can spread this virus, which is a common grass that has made its way from Europe and the Mediterranean.

Maize dwarf mosaic virus

MDMV will appear on young corn leaves as a light and dark mosaic pattern. If the disease progresses, it will grow into narrow streaks along veins and will be evident through dark green blobs against the lighter leaf color. As the infection continues, the leaves will look yellowish-green. Corn infected with MSMV will have excessive tillering, multiple ear shoots, and poor seed sets. If the infection occurs early in the plants' maturity, the plants may develop root and stalk rots and die off.

Corn bacterial infections

Corn can be negatively affected by bacterial infections that can stunt or even kill corn. These can be avoided most of the time by planting resistant varieties.

Bacterial leaf blight

This infection appears as pale-green to yellow, irregular streaks in the leaves. As the disease progresses, the leaves die and dry up. This results in a small yield and opens the plant up to be infected with stalk rot. This type of bacteria can overwinter in corn flea beetles, which spread the disease. The best way to combat the disease is to plant resistant cultivars rather than using pesticides to treat the corn flea beetles.

Bacterial stalk rot

This is an unusual infection because it occurs at ear height rather than coming from the soil. It is transmitted from overhead irrigation where water is sprayed from a lake, stream, or pond. The result of the infection is that the top portion of the plant breaks off. This disease also has a bad odor associated with it. The disease is usually not spread from plant to plant; rather, water or tools often carry it. In order to combat it, you can plant resistant cultivars or use a different water source.

Summary of treatments

Following is a list of steps that can be taken to reduce the damage and loss of yield caused by plant diseases:

1. Crop rotation. Plant a different crop in the plot you had corn in every other year or more.

2. Remove and destroy crop residue. Do not leave any part of the corn stalks, roots, or any other part of the plant over the winter. Remove them with a hoe or shovel and burn them.

3. Find resistant varieties of corn to plant. You can ask your local cooperative extension office what are the best cultivars to plant in your area.

4. Plant the corn at the right time. Ask your seed supplier when the best time to plant the type of corn you are buying seed for in your area is. Do not plant too soon or too late because this may make your plants susceptible to certain types of plant diseases.

5. Do not over-fertilize your corn, because too high a nitrogen level will make your corn susceptible to certain types of diseases.

6. Be sure to harvest your corn at the right time. If you wait too long, you may allow the plant to develop certain types of plant and root rot.

7. Make sure that you store you corn in a cool, dry place.

8. Purchase seed that has been treated for different types of corn diseases.

9. Do not let nematodes get out of control. Treat your soil with nematicides as directed on the bottle. These can be bought at most garden supply stores.

Harvesting corn

You will know that the corn is ready to pick when the ears have become swollen and the corn silk (on top) has turned brown. You can test the corn to see if it is ripe by pulling back the husk and piercing a kernel with your thumbnail. If what comes out of the kernel is milky in color, then the corn is ready to be picked to eat. Be certain that the corn is fully mature in order to use it in brewing. Allow the corn  to remain on the stalk until the husks begin to turn brown. This can take a week or two, depending on how humid the weather is. Pick the corn and remove the husks, then bring the ears inside and allow them to dry in sunlight. When they are completely dry, rub two ears together to remove the dry kernels. You can winnow any debris away from the kernels like you did with barley. Winnowing is the process of removing light plant-material from the grain. This is done by allowing a current of air for blowing out the light pieces of straw. Do this on a day when there is a stiff breeze, or use a fan to create enough airflow. Heavy grain will fall into the bucket, while lighter straw and plant material will be blown away.

Malting corn

You can use corn malt for special styles of beer, like *chicha de jora*. Following are the steps for malting corn that you will use for brewing:

Step 1

Place corn in a large bucket and cover with room temperature water. Allow corn to soak for at least 24 hours.

Step 2

You will need a bucket with holes with a spare bucket underneath, just as you did when malting barley. Fill the bucket with holes with the corn. You do not want to add water to the spare bucket underneath. The holes are to allow the water to drain from the corn daily.

Step 3

Spray the corn with water twice a day, and turn the corn once a day.

Step 4

Continue Step 3 for two days. You corn will begin to germinate or sprout. Allow the sprouts to grow for about five days. They should grow about 2 inches (5 centimeters) long. The corn may get a funny smell, and not all the corn will sprout; this is perfectly normal. The smell is a musty type smell.

Step 5

You can use the kilning oven described under barley in the last chapter, or you can spread sprouted corn on an ungreased cookie sheet and place it in a kitchen oven. If you use the oven, set it on the lowest temperature for electric ovens and on pilot light for gas ovens. It may take six to ten hours to dry.

Step 6

Place dried corn in a sealed container and keep it away from moisture.

Creating Compost From Grains

You will use grains in the brewing process, but instead of just throwing them away you can use them as compost. You can chose to spend upwards to $100 or more on a compost bin at a garden supply store, or you can just use a corner of your garden to compost. It is a natural process that occurs everyday without human intervention. It is the natural process of plant materials decaying and becoming basic minerals and nutrients to be used by a new wave of plants that grow where old plants have died.

The natural process of decay will occur no matter whether you have it in a pile or in a special bin. A bin, pen, or box does make the process a little tidier and can help keep away rodents, pests, and flies.

It does not take too long to transform plant material to compost and can be accomplish in as little as two weeks. The speed of transformation depends on how much material you are composting and how much work you put into it. Large parts of a plant take much longer to break down like stems and branches. This is why used grain works so well, it breaks down quickly. The other thing that will make the process quicker is keeping the pile moist. You can do that by adding some water every few days. It should be moist, not soggy. Compost works better when it is exposed to oxygen, so turning the pile daily will also speed the process of decay. Turning the pile can be done with a pitchfork or shovel. You dig into the pile and then flip the material over. You want to expose the material in the pile to as much air as possible.

The actual process of composting is accomplished by the millions of microorganisms that exist in the soil. They need air, food, and water to live so you need to provide them these materials to convert plant material into usable compost. During the process of composting, these beneficial organisms create heat from digestion. This heat builds up in a compost pile and effectively kills weed seeds and harmful bacteria. As the material is consumed and is used up in the compost pile, the temperature will begin to drop so you need to add more material and oxygen to keep the process alive.

Here are some tips for composting in your yard. These tips work regardless of whether you have the pile in a bin, box, special composting container, or just as a pile in a corner of your yard.

- Be sure that your compost is directly on the soil if not in a composting container.

- Compost does better if it is exposed to direct sunlight.

- Layer your compost like a lasagna. The base of the pile should consist of three to four inches of straw which con come from your harvested grains stalks. This provides good circulation for the compost. The next layers should be three- to four-inch layers of wet green material, like grass clippings from your garden alternated with dry brown material like grains you used for brewing. In addition to grains for the brown material, you can use dry leaves, more straw or even shredded newspaper.

- If you are going to use kitchen scraps of fruits and vegetables in your compost you should add these to the green layer. You should cover these scraps with soil before the next brown layer in order to prevent flies and other insects from being attracted to the pile.

- Once you have layered the pile of even layers of green and brown, you will need to turn the compost with a shovel or pitchfork.

- Be sure to keep the pile moist. Do not allow it to dry out or the beneficial microorganisms that break down the material cannot survive.

- Never add bones, meat, fish, dairy, oils, fats, pet wastes, hardy weeds, diseased plants, or grass that has been treated with herbicides or weed killer. These additions will kill your compost and attract insects and rodents.

Following these simple steps will not only allow you to recycle the grains and other materials in your garden, but also create compost, a nutrient-rich, soil-like organic material that you can use as fertilizer and plant food all around your beer garden.

Do I compost? Absolutely! I have a large compost bin next to my vegetable garden. I add all of our kitchen scraps and grass clippings and garden waste.
— *Annette Pelliccio, founder & CEO, The Happy Gardener, Inc.*

Oat Malt

A number of older, different recipes call for oat malt, but this is no longer the case in modern beer production. Microbrews and home brewers will use flaked or steel-cut oats in some of their beer recipes, but not oat malt, because it is not safe to prepare or create. When these oats are germinating, they can attract poisonous bacteria that create **butanol isomers**, a type of alcohol that is non-digestible and similar to rubbing alcohol or fuel. Therefore, it is not recommended that you grow or try to malt oats for beer. Use store-bought oats instead.

Quinoa

We now move to grains that are used less in making commercial beers, but are great to grow in your garden and experiment with. **Quinoa** is a type of pseudo-cereal, meaning that it is not a true grain or cereal, but it is similar and used in much the same way other grains are used. Quinoa is a chenopod, which makes it related to species such as beets, spinach, and tumbleweeds. Like amaranth, you can eat the leaves like a leaf vegetable, but the edible seeds can be used in beer.

This pseudo-cereal originated in South America in the Andean region and was used as an important food source for about 6,000 years. It is a hardy plant that can grow in mountainous regions, but prefers well-drained soils and long growing seasons.

Quinoa varieties

Name	Maturity	Height	Description
Multi-hued	100-120 days	*5-7 feet (1.5-2.1 m)*	*Seed heads can be mauve, purple, red, yellow, or orange; mid-season variety.*
Faro	100-130 days	*4-6 feet (1.2-1.8 m)*	*Fast growing; drought-tolerant; small, white seeds.*
Dave	90-100 days	*5-6 feet (1.5-1.8 m)*	*Very productive; grows in different elevations; gold seed heads.*
Isuga	90-120 days	*5-7 feet (1.5-2.1 m)*	*High-yield; early maturation; yellow or pink seed heads.*

Planting quinoa

You can begin planting the seeds directly into the ground after the last frost. The soil should be between 55 to 60 degrees Fahrenheit (12 to 15 degrees Celsius). Dig shallow rows with a hoe and place the seeds 4 to 6 inches apart. The rows should be at least 20 inches (51 centimeters) apart from one another.

Water the rows daily until you begin to see seedlings in about a week. After the seedlings have grown ½ inch, thin them to 8 inches (20 centimeters) apart from one another. You do not need to overwater the plants, as they are drought tolerant. They only need about 10 inches (25 centimeters) of water for the entire growing season. By midsummer, you will begin to see seed heads like those described for amaranth.

Harvesting quinoa

After the first frost in autumn, quinoa will be ready to harvest. After the frost, the heads will begin to dry out. Allow them to dry for a week, and then cut the seed heads off. Once you have cut the seed heads, you will need to hang them in a dry place with good air circulation like an attic or barn. You will need to allow the seed heads to become completely dry; they should become brittle to the touch.

Malting quinoa

Step 1

Place the grain in a large jar, fill with room temperature water to cover grain, and cover with cheesecloth for 12 hours. After this period, rinse the grain with cold water and drain. Place the jar containing the grain in a warm, dark place. Continue to rinse the grain at least three times a day.

Step 2

Allow grain to sit for three to four days. Keep an eye on the grain and check to see if the acrospires have formed. You will see a white circle around the top of the grain when this occurs. You will notice that the center of the seed has darkened, and there may be some root beginning to grow from the seed. Once this has occurred, proceed to Step 3.

Step 3

In this step, you will kiln the grain to dry it out. *This can be done in a regular oven, but the kiln described in Chapter 2 will be more effective.* Place the quinoa seed evenly on a cookie sheet or any other shallow pan. Set the oven on its lowest setting for two to six hours. If you have a gas oven, just leave on the pilot light. For every pound (.45 kilograms) of grain, you will yield about 6 ounces (171 milligrams) of malt for brewing.

Allow the grain to cool; store in a cool dry place, like a closet, for a week before using.

Rye

The reasons for not growing and creating rye malt at home are similar to the reasons given for oats, except that rye can be even more dangerous. You can buy rye malt that has been created by professionals to create beers like Finnish sahti or German roggen-bier. *In Appendix B, you can find a list of resources to buy rye.*

Sorghum

This grain is often used as a feeder for animals. It is either cultivated as a food for animals or allowed to grow in a pasture for domesticated animals to eat. Sorghum grows well in warmer climates and is native to tropical and subtropical regions in the South West Pacific and Australia. That is not to say that cannot be grown elsewhere. It is cultivated in Central America, South Asia, and Africa. According to the U.S. Grains Council, it is the "fifth most important cereal crop grown in the world."

Sorghum can be used for people food in the form of grain, sorghum syrup or sorghum molasses, and, of course, it is used in alcohol beverages such as beer. In 2006, Anheuser-Busch Company created a beer called Redbridge in response to people that had Celiac disease, which is wheat and barley gluten intolerance. It contains neither wheat nor barley and is a lager made exclusively with sorghum.

A liquor produced in China called maotai is made from fermented and distilled sorghum.

Sorghum varieties

Name	Maturity	Height	Description
White African	*100-120 days*	*10-12 feet (3-3.7 m)*	*White seeds; very productive; black-and-white seed heads; sweet variety.*
Mennonite	*90-95 days*	*7-10 feet (2.1-3 m)*	*Sweet variety; red seeds; orange-red seed heads*

Planting sorghum

Check your farmer's almanac for the frost-free date. A week before this date is when you will plant your sorghum. If you want to start the plants indoors, you can begin three to four weeks before the frost-free date and then plant the seedlings directly.

If planting seeds directly, you will want to hoe a shallow trench. Place the seeds at least 7 inches (18 centimeters) from one another. The space between the rows should be 2 to 3 feet (.6 to .9 meters). Water the garden daily until you begin to see seedlings. If you started the seedlings indoors, you will need to space them 14 inches (35 centimeters) apart; if you planted them outdoors, you will need to thin the seedlings until they are 14 inches (35 centimeters) apart.

Sorghum is like quinoa in that it is very drought resistant and heat resistant. You will begin to see the seed heads by midsummer, although the grain will not be mature until late summer or early autumn.

Harvesting sorghum

You will begin to see the seed heads dry out in early autumn. The process of harvesting is much the same as it was with quinoa. You will need to cut the seed heads and hang them in a dry place where they can get plenty of air in order to completely dry. Once they are dry, you will need to use small garden clippers to cut off the tassels. You can then rub the grain off between your hands. You then can winnow the remaining chaff or debris as with other grains.

Malting sorghum

Step 1

Place the grain in a large jar, fill with water to cover grain, and cover with cheesecloth for 18 hours. After this period, rinse the grain with cold water and drain. Place the jar containing the grain in a warm, dark place. Continue to rinse the grain at least three times a day.

Step 2

Allow grain to sit for three to four days. Keep an eye on the grain, and look to see if the acrospires have formed. Acrospires will grow ¾ to 2 inches (1.9 to 5 centimeters). Once this has occurred, proceed to Step 3.

Step 3

In this step, you will kiln the grain to dry it out. Place the sorghum seed evenly on a cookie sheet or any other shallow pan. Set the oven on its lowest setting for six to 12 hours. (If you have a gas oven, just leave on the pilot light). Allow the grain to cool, and store in a sealed container for a week before using.

Spelt

Spelt is a species similar to wheat. In the Bronze to medieval times, spelt was an important food in parts of Europe. Spelt is used today in the form of matzo in the Jewish holiday of Passover. Matzo is unleavened bread, which means that it does not rise and is cracker-like. It is used in Bavaria in a specialty beer called Dinkel beer. Beer is not the only alcoholic beverage that spelt is used in. In Denmark, there is a special gin made with spelt. In Poland, spelt is used to make Vodka.

Spelt varieties

Name	Maturity	Description
Champ	120 days	Leaf-rust resistant; strong stems;

Planting spelt

Planting spelt is very similar to planing barley. The soil should be dry and the seeds should be sown in early spring. You should spread the seeds over soil that you have raked smooth and then once you have evenly scattered the seeds you can use the rake gently to scratch them into the soil. Once you have done this, water them lightly by sprinkling the water. Once the seeds have been planted, they do not require much care and are hardy plants.

Harvesting spelt

By the end of the summer, the spelt will be ready to harvest. To harvest you will need to cut the stalks, then lay them like barley in piles and allow them to dry out for at least a week. Once they are dry, you need to thresh the grain using the same method you did with barley by placing the stalks on a drop cloth or sheet. Once you have removed the grain you will need to pour it into a bucket and winnow it the same way you did with barely. You can store the spelt in a burlap sack in a cool, dry place. You should wait until the weather cools to malt the spelt.

Malting spelt

Step 1

Place the grain in a large jar, fill with water to cover grain, and cover with cheesecloth for 12 hours. After this period, you will want to rinse the grain with cold water and drain. Place the jar containing the grain in a warm, dark place. Continue to rinse the grain at least three times a day.

Step 2

Allow grain to sit for two to three days. Keep an eye on the grain and look to see if the acrospires have formed. Once the acrospires are the same length as the grain, proceed to Step 3.

Step 3

In this step, you will kiln the grain to dry it out. Place the **spelt** seed in an even layer on a cookie sheet or any other shallow pan. Set the kitchen oven on its lowest setting for two to six hours.

If you have a gas oven, just leave on the pilot light. For every pound (.45 kilograms) of grain, you will yield about 6 ounces (171 milligrams) of malt for brewing.

Allow the grain to cool, and store for at least a week before using.

Wheat

Wheat is so similar to barley that the planting and harvesting directions contained in Chapter 2 can be applied to wheat. While planting and harvesting are similar, the malting of wheat does present some unique challenges. Unlike barley, wheat does not have a thick outer hull. This means that the time for steeping is shorter. The other difference is that the acrospire grows outside the grain, which makes turning it more difficult because of the danger of damaging the acrospire, which would kill the individual grains. The most difficult challenge is that it takes hours of kilning to malt. This can make it difficult to process.

Malting wheat

Step 1: Cleansing the grains

It is a good idea to weigh your grain before you begin the malting process. This will give you a baseline weight you can use to determine when the grain is dry again, as water will be added to the grain during the malting process.

Once you have weighed the grain, rinse it. This removes any left-over debris, straw, chaff, or weed seeds before you begin malting the grain. The easiest way to do this is to place the grain in one of the buckets. Make sure there is plenty of space for water to ensure that you can submerge the grains. Gently stir the grain and allow it to settle. The grain is heavy and will sink to the bottom, while debris will float. You can use a large spoon to skim off the debris. Put the debris in the trash or compost if you like, but do not put into the sink, as this can clog it.

Place the bucket with the holes inside into the extra 5-gallon bucket. Pour the grain and water into the bucket with the holes, and allow water to drain into the bucket underneath. Return the grains into the original bucket. Refill the bucket with water, and make sure the grains are submerged again.

Step 2: Steeping the grains

Allow the grains to stay in the water for at least 72 hours. Make sure that the grains are covered with about ½ gallon (2 degrees Lovibond) of water during this period, and that the temperature remains at 50 degrees Fahrenheit (10 degrees Celsius). You will have to change the water after the initial two hours and then every 12 hours after that. Change the water the same way you did in Step 1 by using the bucket with the holes inside the extra bucket.

If you are using the aquarium stone, place it in the bottom of the bucket and allow it to run. This permits the grains to be aerated and, therefore, instead of changing the grains every 12 hours, you will only have to change them every 24 hours.

Once you have steeped the grains for 48 hours, you will notice that the grains are swollen when they have taken on water and expanded to 150 percent of the grain's original volume.

Step 3: Germinating the grains

Drain the bucket again as you have done in the past two steps, using the bucket with the holes and the spare bucket underneath. This process should be done in an area that is about 50 degrees Fahrenheit (10 degrees Celsius), and this temperature should remain constant. The grains will get to about 59 degrees Fahrenheit to about 65 degrees Fahrenheit (12 degrees to 15 degrees Celsius), but should never exceed 68 degrees Fahrenheit (20 degrees Celsius).

Make sure you do not cut off the air to the aquarium stone when you place the bucket of grain with the holes in the bottom inside the bucket with water.

If you do not use the aquarium stone, the setup is the same, but you will have to turn the grains often.

It will take about three days for the grains to complete germination. You will be able to see the acrospire because it is on the outside of the wheat. The acrospire should be about ⅔ of the length of the grain. When it reaches that point, progress to Step 4.

Step 4: Couching the malt

Once the acrospires have reached ⅔ the length of the grain, you will give the grain a carbon dioxide bath to stop the growth process. This lets the enzymes convert the starch into fermentable sugar. In the last step, you released the starches by allowing the acrospire to grow; now, it is time to convert that starch.

The process is simple. Attach the lid on top of the bucket with holes on it. You will turn off pump attached to the aquarium stone, and you will need to turn the grains to prevent heat build-up at least once a day. Make sure that this stops the growth of the acrospire. If you see that it is still growing, quickly go to Step 5. If not, allow the grain to couch for one to three additional days.

Step 5: Kilning the malt

In this step, you will be drying out the grain again. *If you do not have a drying cabinet as described in the Chapter 2, you should use your oven.* You can use a cookie sheet to dry the grains. Spread them evenly and stir them occasionally as they dry. It takes about 48 hours to dry out 5 pounds (2.3 kilograms) of malt at a temperature of 178 degrees Fahrenheit (80 degrees Celsius).

Chapter 4

Hops

"Brewers enjoy working to make beer as much as drinking beer instead of working."
— **Harold Rudolph, a 19th century artist from Louisiana**

What are Hops?

Humulus lupulus, or hops, is a primary flavoring ingredient in beer. Hops impart a taste that can be referred to as crisp, herbal, bitter, or even palate cleansing. The smell of hops in beer is a somewhat herbal or grassy aroma. This vining plant produces clusters of flowers that are referred to as strobiles or cones. This is the part of the plant used in beer production. The resin in the hops flower contains two types of acids: alpha and beta.

The **alpha acids** offer an antibacterial effect to beer, but do not affect brewing yeast that is essential for the fermentation of beer. The bitter flavor in beer is also the result of alpha acids in hops. These acids are released in the boiling of the hops during the preparation of beer. These are often referred to as bittering hops. Bittering hops have to be boiled an extra amount of time — between 60 and 90 minutes — because the alpha acids must be **isomerized**. Hops can range from 4 to 15 percent alpha acids.

The full potential of the bitter compounds to emerge in the flavor of a beer is through the process of isomerization. Alpha acids in hops are not very water-soluble and must be extracted from the hops. Placing hops in the wort is not enough. **Isomerization** is a chemical process that occurs when the resins are boiled in the wort, which is slightly acidic. This transforms the alpha acids into water-soluble, iso-alpha acids, which become part of the beer and add to its bitter taste. When reading about hops, you will see "% AA" next to the name. This refers to a hops alpha acid percentage. The percentage of alpha acids helps determine what their bittering potential is in a beer. They do not contribute much to the aroma of a beer. The bitterness of a beer is measured in units called **International Bitterness Units (IBUs)**.

The other type of acid in hop flowers, **beta acid**, does not have much effect on the taste of beer. Aroma hops often have lower alpha level acids, usually less than 5 percent. Instead, they are more responsible for the bitter, herbal smell in beer. Hops that contain high levels of beta acids are often referred to as aroma hops and are added the last couple of minutes of the boiling of the wort. The reason they are added so late in the boiling process is to prevent the oils from evaporating. These oils contribute to the smell of hops in beer. Aroma hops should be boiled for about three minutes to release the oils from hops, but not evaporate or change them.

Sometimes aroma hops are even added after boiling the wort through a technique called **dry hopping**. In this process, hops are added to the wort after it has cooled. The oils that are released are myrcene, humulene, caryophyllene, and farnesene, which contribute to 60 to 80 percent of the essential oils for most hop varieties.

In addition to the potential of bitterness that hops can impart in a beer, they can also offer a "hop" flavor, which is referred to as herbal, grassy, or even citrusy. Some aroma hops, such as Cascade hops, can impart flavor, and are therefore used as flavoring hops. These are cooked a shorter time than bittering hops, but slightly longer than aroma hops — about 15 minutes. Many beers use these flavoring hops to add to the depth of flavor in a beer.

In addition to their use in beer, bittering hops are also a common component in herbal medicine and a variety of other drinks. They are used in medicine for their natural antibiotic flavor, and it is believed they can help a person with insomnia or upset stomach. The flavor of the hops cones can range from bitter to tangy. The key to the flavor is how they are prepared and used.

Hops have an interesting history; they were documented as early as the eighth and ninth centuries as a crop grown in Bavaria (old Germany). At that time, hops would have been used as a medicinal and flavoring additive. But it would not be hard to imagine that brewers would begin to use them in their beer recipes as well.

In our modern world, brewers use the bitterness of hops to counterbalance the sweetness of malt. Recipes that strive for smoothness have a balanced amount of bitter and sweet, while some seek the bitter flavor in greater proportion.

Hops belong in the same family as stinging nettles. Stinging nettles are a plant that contains leaves and stems covered in stinging hairs with tips that act like a hypodermic needle when touched and inject several chemicals: acetylcholine, histamine, 5-HT or serotonin, and formic acid. When injected, these chemicals create a painful and itchy sting. The effect can last anywhere from few minutes to as long as a week.

Hops grow each year from the perennial base root or stump; the stems or vines of the hops plant will come back year after year. These vines naturally twine around strings, posts, bars, fences, and just about anything else they come in contact with. These vines grow either horizontally or vertically and can sometimes reach a length of 40 feet. The vines are prickly, giving you a hint as to why they share a family with stinging nettles. Hops, however, do not have stinging barbs. The vines themselves are very tough and grow into a resilient fiber that has also been used to make cloth or paper as they are closely related to hemp. These stems or vines are more commonly referred to as bines.

The leaves of the hops plant are lobed in the shape of a heart and occur across from one another on the stem. These leaves have jagged or toothed edges and are dark green when the plant is healthy. When they are not healthy, they may look pale, shriveled or wilted.

The flowers of the hops plants grow at the axles of the leaves — the place where the leaf is attached to the stem. Hops are dioecious, with male flowers exclusive to male plants and female flowers exclusive to female plants. Only female hops plants are cultivated as a flavor additive in beer. Only the female plants create **strobiles** or cones.

The cones of a female hops plant are usually more than an inch long, oblong, and a yellowy-green color. The cones grow in clusters with the fruit, or **achene**, at the base of each cone. The fruits of the female hops plant are sprinkled with clear, yellowy glands that appear as a powder substance or pollen; the more of the powdery substance, the better. This powder contains the ingredient **lupulin**, a resin that contributes to the bitter flavor in beer.

The portion of the plant that you will buy planting is called a rhizome. A rhizome is the base stem of a plant that is located beneath the ground and produces new shoots and roots. Hops rhizomes multiply underground in the same way lilies, cannas, and asparagus do. When dug up and separated, each new segment of the original rhizome will become a new rhizome that can be planted. You will need to plant hops rhizomes in your garden in order to grow hop vines.

Hops are produced commercially in what are called hop fields, hop yards, or hop gardens. The hops plant is an aggressive vine that grows vigorously up twine or strings that can support their weight. A wide variety of hops plants are produced all over the world today. Each plant has its own flavor and is produced for a particular style of beer. These variations occur because certain varieties of hops grew naturally in some areas of the world, and beer makers used what was made available to them. Hops are grown around the world, but can be found most commonly in Germany and the United States, especially in the state of Washington.

Where Hops can be Grown

People sometimes try to grow regular hop varieties on low trellis systems. Yields using this system might be acceptable if you just need a handful of hops on a yearly basis. However, it is critical that gardeners grow hops on as tall a trellis as they can realistically handle. In addition, hops grow and produce best above the 35th parallel with best yields obtained from the 45th to 50th parallel. This means that crops in regions such as the Southeast or Southwest will not produce well. Hops have a dormancy and chilling requirement for flower production the following year. This means that hops will most likely not flower when soil temperatures never get below 40 degrees Fahrenheit for six to eight weeks. Many places that might work for hop production based upon day length in the summer may not produce well unless they are grown at high elevations to achieve the chilling requirement (dormancy).

*AA = alpha acid

Name	Origin	AA (%)	Type
Ahtanum	U.S.	6	Aroma
Amarillo Gold	U.S.	8.5	Aroma
Aquila	U.S.	6.5	Aroma
Bramling Cross	U.K.	6	Aroma
Challenger	U.K.	7.5	Aroma
Crystal	U.S.	3.5	Aroma

Name	Origin	AA (%)	Type
Fuggles	U.K.	4.5	Aroma
Glacier	U.S.	5.6	Aroma
Goldings, B. C.	Canada	5	Aroma
Goldings, East Kent (EK)	U.K.	5	Aroma
Hallertauer	Germany	4.8	Aroma
Hallertauer, Hersbrucker	Germany	4	Aroma
Hallertauer, Mittelfrueh	Germany	4	Aroma
Liberty	U.S.	4.3	Aroma
Mt. Hood	U.S.	6	Aroma
Progress	U.K.	6.3	Aroma
Saaz	Czech Rep	4	Aroma
Santiam	US	6	Aroma
Select Spalt	Germany	4.8	Aroma
Spalter	Germany	4.5	Aroma
Strisselspalt	France	4	Aroma
Styrian Goldings	Slovenia	5.4	Aroma

Name	Origin	AA (%)	Type
Tettnang	Germany	4.5	Aroma
Ultra	U.S.	3	Aroma
Vanguard	U.S.	5.5	Aroma
Whitbread Golding Var (WGV)	U.K.	6	Aroma
Willamette	U.S.	5	Aroma
Admiral	U.K.	14.8	Bittering
Banner	U.S.	10	Bittering
Brewers Gold	U.K.	8	Bittering
Bullion	U.K.	8	Bittering
Centennial	U.S.	10	Bittering
Chinook	U.S.	13	Bittering
Cluster	U.S.	7	Bittering
Columbia	U.K.	5	Bittering
Columbus (Tomahawk)	U.S.	14	Bittering
Comet	U.S.	9.5	Bittering
Eroica	U.S.	13	Bittering
Galena	U.S.	13	Bittering

Name	Origin	AA (%)	Type
Green Bullet	New Zealand	13.5	Bittering
Herald	U.K.	12	Bittering
Horizon	U.S.	12	Bittering
Lublin	Poland	5	Bittering
Magnum	Germany	14	Bittering
Nugget	U.S.	13	Bittering
Pacific Gem	New Zealand	15	Bittering
Perle	Germany	8	Bittering
Phoenix	U.K.	8	Bittering
Pilgrim	U.K.	11.5	Bittering
Pride of Ring-wood	Australia	9	Bittering
Sun	U.S.	14	Bittering
Super Alpha	New Zealand	13	Bittering
Target	U.K.	11	Bittering
Tradition	Germany	6	Bittering
Zeus	U.S.	14	Bittering
Cascade	U.S.	5.5	Both

Name	Origin	AA (%)	Type
First Gold	*U.K.*	*7.5*	*Both*
Hallertauer, New Zealand	*New Zealand*	*8.5*	*Both*
Northdown	*U.K.*	*8.5*	*Both*
Northern Brewer	*Germany*	*8.5*	*Both*
Orion	*Germany*	*7.3*	*Both*
Pioneer	*U.K.*	*9*	*Both*
Southern Cross	*New Zealand*	*13*	*Both*
Sterling	*U.S.*	*7.5*	*Both*
Sticklebract	*New Zealand*	*13.5*	*Both*
Warrior	*U.S.*	*15*	*Both*

"Hops developed by USA Hop Breeding programs — both public and private — are the best varieties to grow. There are quite a few available, and the number of varieties developed by these programs increases each year. Varieties developed by other countries typically do not grow as well as the USA-developed varieties due to environmental differences between locations where breeding of the variety took place."
— Dr. John Henning, program leader, Hop Genetics and Breeding Program, USDA-ARS-FSRC

A general rule of thumb is that hops can be grown in hardiness zones four through eight. Many varieties of hops vines available for purchase are hardy to these zones and even the extreme zones as well. Check with your local agricultural cooperative extension office or at a beer supply shop to determine the specific varieties that may grow well in your area. *There are a number of sources in Appendix B for hop distributors.* If you live in an area such as the Pacific Northwest, you may be lucky enough to get hops from a local commercial grower. You can do a search on the Internet to find the contact information for local hop growers in your area.

You will need to purchase the hop rhizome, or root part of the hop to plant. You can begin purchasing rhizomes in early spring. Here is a list of things to look for when purchasing rhizomes from a local grower or an online supplier.

- They should be plump. They should not be withered or dried out.

- They should have a healthy look, not dead and diseased.

- You should be able to see rootlets and white sprouts.

- The texture should be firm to the touch. There should be no soft spots and will not compress easily when firmly squeezed between your fingers.

If your rhizomes are not of high quality, you should contact the distributor about replacement or a refund. When the rhizomes arrive at your home, you should keep them in a cool, dry place before you plant them. You can wrap them in damp sawdust, peat moss, or newspaper to keep them moist.

Choose a variety that is proven to produce well in your specific area. The soil composition and year-round climate are critical factors that impact the success of your crop and season. You may need to experiment a bit with different varieties. The person selling the rhizomes should be able to tell you what varieties will grow the best. A rule of thumb with hops or any other outdoor plant is that they should be able to live the way we do. This means a plant should be able to grow and survive in the average conditions where you live. If you notice that the hop plant looks sickly, brown, diseased, or is full of insects, you may want to pull it up and try a different variety. This may take some trial and error; so try more than one variety the first year.

For your first year, plant one row instead of eight rows. Your first year is an experiment to see what varieties will grow the best in your area. You do not want to invest a lot of money on rhizomes until you are sure that the particular variety you want to grow will survive.

Choosing the Right Hop Yard Site

A hop yard is the traditional name for a hop garden site. Hop plants will require, at minimum, 120 days without frost to produce the blooms you will require. In addition to the temperature, your hop plants need copious amounts of sunlight. The vines will require direct sun for at least 15 hours each day. These factors limit the hardiness zones to four to eight, or between the 35 degrees and 55 degrees latitude. The optimum growing season for your hop crop begins with a very wet spring followed by a steadily warm summer. If you live in an area that has a history of drier summers, be prepared to have an irrigation system that will provide your vines with consistent hydration for the duration of your growing season. Hops use a lot of water to grow, but you need to be sure you do not over water. If you waterlog the vines roots, you will kill the plant.

While the hop vine is growing, the hop hills should be evenly moist. You can check this by hand. It should be wet, but not at the level of mud. When hop plants are first planted and during the dry season, you should water your plants every day. You can buy easy-to-install irrigation systems from your local hardware or garden supply store for about $100.

When choosing a hop yard, you need to think about the amount of space you will need. Hops are planted in small mounds or hills with the plants spaced 2 ½ to 3 feet (.8 to 1 meter) away from one another. The hills will be 6 to 7 inches tall and about a foot across. You will plant one or two hop rhizomes per hill. If you planted five hills you would require a hop yard of 3 feet wide and 15 feet long (1 meter by 5 meters). Hops vines do not require a great deal of square footage. You can even grow a hop plant in a container; you would need at least a 5-gallon container to support the root growth.

Soil preparation

The soil in your hop garden is another critical factor in the success of your vines. Your hop yard should have a 2-foot depth of good, workable soil. Ideally, you should locate an area with a sandy loam — a loose and workable soil that will stay well drained during the growing season. Test your soil prior to planting your vines to determine the nutrient qualities that naturally occur and what types of fertilizers can be added. Avoid more saline (salty) or alkaline (high pH) soils, or your vines will grow poorly and have limited production. Most hops grow the best in a soil with a pH of 6 to 7.5. Your vines will need nitrogen, potassium, phosphorus, calcium, boron, zinc, molybdenum, and phosphate. Without the proper amount of nutrients, your vines' growth will become stunted, and your plants will take on a pale color.

Using good compost will provide your hops with all of the nutrients it should need. You should spread compost about 3 inches (8 centimeters) thick over the hop hills before planting, and you should not need to add many nutrients afterward.

The following chart can be used not only for altering the pH in the soil for hops, but also can be used for all the plants in your beer garden. Each of these soil additives can be purchased at a well-stocked hardware or garden supply store.

Material	What it does	How much to use
Wood Ash	*Wood ash will increase the pH in soil. It will also add magnesium, potassium, and other nutrients.*	*You can apply 1 to 3 pounds (454 g to 1.3 kg) of wood ash per 100 square feet (9 sq. m) of garden space*
Sulfur	*Sulfur will lower the pH in soil. This is good to use in soil that is too alkaline.*	*1 pound (454 g) of sulfur per 100 square feet (9 sq. m) will lower the pH by one point in sandy soil. You will have to add 1 ½ pounds (680 g) in loamy soil and 2 pounds (908 g) in clay soil.*

Material	What it does	How much to use
Phosphate (hard rock)	*Hard rock phosphate will raise the pH one point or more when applied. It will also add phosphorus and iron to the soil as well.*	*You will need to add 10 pounds (4.5 kg) to raise the pH at least one point in 100 square foot (9 sq. m) of soil.*
Phosphate (colloidal)	*This also raises the pH in soil and is a great source of phosphorus.*	*The addition of 5 pounds of colloidal Phosphate is needed to raise the pH by a point in 100 square feet (9 sq. m) of soil.*
Dolomite limestone	*Dolomite limestone is used to raise the pH in soil. It also adds a significant amount of magnesium. If you do not need magnesium in your soil, you can substitute calcitic limestone.*	*The addition of 7 pounds. (3 kg) of either type of limestone will raise the pH by one point in 100 square feet (9 sq. m) of predominantly clay soil. In sandy soil, you will need to use 2 to 3 pounds. of limestone (908 g to 1.3 kg), and in loamy soil, you will need 6 pounds (2.7 kg) of limestone.*
Bone meal	*Bone meal will raise the pH of soil, and it contains phosphorus.*	*In order to raise the pH in 100 square feet (9 sq. m) of soil, you will need 3 pounds (1.3 kg) of bone meal.*

Material	What it does	How much to use
Compost	*Average store-bought compost will lower the pH in alkaline soils, but can also raise the pH in more acidic soils. Read the package to determine which type of compost you need and what it is used for, as there are different types. In addition to changing the pH of soil, compost will also add needed nutrients to plants.*	*For 100 square feet (9 sq. m), you will need 1 to 2 bushels of compost to raise or lower the pH by at least one point.*

"We add all of our veggie and fruit scraps to our composter, so every summer we have lots of watermelon and cantaloupe rinds that are thrown in there. Every summer, we get at least one watermelon or cantaloupe plant that has self-seeded from inside the composter and grown out the bottom of it. These plants always produce the best and biggest fruit because they are growing inside that wonderful compost soil. My kids get so excited every year to see what is going to come growing out the bottom of the composter."

— *Annette Pelliccio, founder & CEO, The Happy Gardener, Inc.*

Once you have determined the variety that is best for your location, and know what your ideal soil chemistry should look like, prepare a place for your vines to be planted.

Currently, the only hop varieties available to the public are non-dwarf or regular-trellis hop varieties. These varieties grow best on trellis systems that are approximately 18 feet tall above ground. This means the poles would be about 22 feet long with 4 feet underground.

Your hops vines will grow up on vertical supports to heights that can reach 40 feet, if they have the space to do so. The higher the vine, the more hops that can be harvested. Most small production hop yards like the one you will plant usually are not that high. An ideal location for planting your vines would be along a fence line or garage — a location that you will not mind having a 10- to 20-foot vertical plant growing all summer long. The most common system for supporting hops vines on a small scale is to allow them to vine up a sturdy trellis that is a minimum of 10 feet high.

Because of the hard work you will be putting into creating your trellis, you will want to create it only once. Therefore, choose the right materials, spend the time to make sure that poles are firmly planted, and that the **guy wires** — the galvanized wires that the hop vines will be growing on — are securely attached to the poles and anchors in the ground.

You may be lucky enough to have existing structures, such as trees or the wall of a building, where you can attach the guy wires by screwing in and installing a hook. If you do not have these structures available, then you will have to dig and install some poles. A couple of different trellis systems are mentioned in this book. These are the simplest to construct and, if installed correctly, will be sturdy and last for many plantings. The trellis system should be sturdy enough to support your weight on a ladder, since you will need to use a ladder to harvest the hops.

Tent Pole Trellis System

Your goal in this support system is to create a teepee shape with your hops growing around it, each plant growing up its own guy wire to the top of the pole, where they will all come together. If you have a rectangular plot that is long and narrow, then instead of an area that you can create a circle, grow your plants in a row with the pole situated behind them. Each guy wire will lead from the plants to the top of the pole, creating a fan shape instead of a circle. Both configurations will work equally as well.

An important factor to consider as you construct your trellis system is how to get the wires down. You must be able to remove the wires laden with vines from the top of your support structure and lower them to the ground for harvesting; thus, you need to gain free access to the top of the trellis using a ladder, and then be able to detach the wire at the top. This may mean leaving extra space between a few plants or allowing for side access to the top of the support.

Some homeowners use hops gardens that have incorporated their vines into sunshades for patios, places for children to play, or as privacy devices to separate homes and backyards from the neighbors' view. No matter where you set up your plot and your vine support system, you can anticipate lush, green vines growing for your pleasure all summer long.

Here are the step-by-step directions for creating a tent-pole trellis:

Supplies

- A 16-foot (4.8-meter) wood or metal pole for every six hops plants

- A post-hole digger (or shovel)

- A large, flat stone to fit in bottom of hole (1 foot in diameter or slightly more)

- A small bag of gravel or small rocks

- Anchors (These are metal stakes that are driven into the ground and have a eye hook to attach wire to.)

- 3 ring bolts (galvanized)

- $\frac{3}{16}$-inch galvanized wire (enough to hold the pole in place, 7 feet from the pole)

- Carpenter's level

- Heavy-duty twine (optional if you intend to plant four to six hops plants)

1. For a tent pole trellis, you can attach up to six plants evenly spaced to one pole. You will need a 16-foot (4.8-meter) pole made from wood or metal. If using wood, you will want to choose locust, cedar, or spruce because these woods will not rot; often, you can find the right size, but if you cannot, you can purchase the pole from a large hardware store that can cut it to size and even deliver it, if needed. If you want to use a metal pole, consider using a section of aluminum irrigation pipe. Again, a hardware store can cut it to the right size.

2. Using a post-hole digger or a shovel, you will need to dig a 3-foot (1-meter) deep hole.

3. Place the large flat stone in the bottom of the hole. The hole will need to be wide enough to accommodate the stone so that it lays flat.

4. Place pole in the center of the hole and place gravel or small rocks around it in the hole to hold it in place.

5. Use the level to make sure the pole is straight. You may need to place it on top of the pole and make adjustments until the bubble on the level is between the two marks that indicate that the pole is straight up and down.

6. Attach three ring bolts equal distant from one another near the top of the pole. Tie a guy wire to each of the bolts.

7. Attach the other end of the guy wires to the anchor stakes that are seven feet away from the pole in three directions.

8. You can then create between three and six hills inside the ring of anchors. You will use the guy wires to train three of your hops plants. If you intend to plant six, you can add three more eye bolts to the top of the pole and three more anchors in the spaces between the original three. These original three provide support for the pole; therefore need the galvanized wire. You can replace the wire with strong twine for the three additional guy wires.

9. Plant and create hills for each of the hops rhizomes. *This will be explained in detail below.*

Straight Pole Trellis

The second common setup for a hops trellis is the straight pole trellis. This uses two 13-foot poles that are placed on either side of the hop yard you have chosen, or about 25 feet (8 meters) from one another. The poles will be buried in the ground about 3 feet deep. They should be buried with the tops of the poles facing away from one another at a about a 15-degree angle. Between these two poles thread a guy wire through holes that are drilled about a foot from the top.

Once you have placed the poles in the ground using a post-hole digger, you will pass the wire through the holes you made and anchor the ends to the ground. A great way to anchor the wire is to tie the end to a cement cinder block, and then bury the cinder block a foot or two underground a few feet away from each pole.

Planting the rhizomes

Once you have the guy-wire attached and the poles buried, it is time to plant the rhizomes.

Your rhizomes will be planted the long way, or horizontally, in the ground. You need to identify the shoots and roots. The white shoots will be planted upward and the spindly roots down underneath.

Once you have identified where you want to plant the rhizome, you will create a small mound about 8 inches high. It must be big enough to hold your rhizome. In the top of the mound, you will dig a small trench of about 6 inches (15 centimeters) deep to lay the rhizome in, and then cover each rhizome with about 2 inches (5 centimeters) of soil.

Remember that your mounds must be about 2 ½ feet to 3 feet (80 centimeters to 1 meter) apart from one another. You can plant one or two rhizomes in each hill; however, they should be the same variety to prevent any confusion.

Once you have all the rhizomes planted, you should cover each hill with about 1 to 2 inches (2.3 to 5 centimeters) of mulch or straw. In between the mounds, you should spread more mulch or straw about 3 to 6 inches deep (8 to 15 centimeters). This mulch protects against weeds growing on or in between your mounds.

For the first few weeks, keep the mounds moist with water. The water can be shallow because it will take time for the root systems to grow. As the hops grow through the season, continue to add mulch, as it does decay. Mulch will keep weeds from growing and discourage pests while keeping the ground moist.

Once you have planted your rhizomes, sink a metal stake in the ground and attach a wire — or, better yet, jute twine — from the stake to the guy wire. Jute twine is biodegradable, so at the end of the season, you can throw it in the compost along with the vines after the hops have been harvested. Attach the twine or wire in a V-shape between the stake and the guy wire. Loop the twine over the top and hook it to the next stake in a V-shape, and so on until all the stakes have a two strings coming from them to the guy wire. You can tie off the ends of the twine at each of the poles.

Training the vines

Once your hops are established, they will begin to grow about a foot a week. This means they can grow about 30 feet each growing season. You want to make sure that you train your vines and do not allow them to overwhelm the mounds. The goal is to make sure all of the energy of the plant is used for growing the hop cones, which is the part of the plant you will be using.

Once the vines begin to grow, choose the two healthiest vines from each rhizome to be trained, and prune or remove the rest of the vines to be composted. The chosen vines should be trained to grow up the guy wire string by winding them around it. As your vines grow, your primary goal is to allow air to flow along the base of the plants and keep your vines from becoming tangled with each other. Tangled vines redistribute the weight of the plants and could bring your entire trellis system crashing to the ground.

At midsummer, prune the bottom 4 feet of each of your vines so that the foliage has been stripped, and air can flow freely among the roots. Cut the leaves and extra vines from this area using a pair of garden clippers. This will aid in disease prevention and ensure your irrigation system reaches every plant in your plot. During the height of the summer, it will be to your advantage to be able to see the bottom of your plants and have room to inspect the growing foliage for diseased leaves and insect pests. June bugs and aphids, in particular, will be drawn to your hops. Wash them off your plants with water straight from the hose, or use pesticide chemicals, if you choose. If you do use chemical pesticides, remember to wash each harvested bud carefully to prevent any residue from contaminating your beer.

"The greatest pests that a grower faces typically are fungal patho-gens such as powdery mildew and downy mildew. Recently developed USDA-ARS varieties such as Newport and Mount Rainier carry resistance — either strong or moderate — to both diseases."

— Dr. John Henning, program leader, Hop Genetics
and Breeding Program, USDA-ARS-FSRC

The Great Hops Shortage

In 2007, the perfect storm hit beer makers worldwide. The acreage used for hops production was rapidly decreasing, in stark contrast to the increase in craft brew production, independent breweries, and home brewers. Weather had caused crop failure across Europe, putting pressure on other growers, and a fire destroyed a Yakima, Washington, warehouse along with the 2 million pounds of hops being stored inside.

The result of so many devastating factors occurring all at once made the price of hops skyrocket. Just like gas, prices rise when crude oil supplies are threatened; the hops market reacted in the same way. Even beer prices increased to cover the cost of production.

Up to the year 2007, hops prices had held steady at about $2 or $3 per pound. As brewers began to feel the pinch of the shortage, demand forced the price of hops to as much as $30 per pound in some cases. Farmers, of course, reacted to the shortage and the fantastic profit that could be had from selling crops, and began to add acreage wherever it was feasible.

The boomerang effect of increasing the hops production to satisfy a shortage was that by 2008 and 2009, hops became abundantly accessible. During 2008, the hops crops were sometimes left unharvested and unused due to the glut in the market. The market has since rebounded to a stable price with an even supply and demand.

This is just one reason why you should grow your own hops at home; you will never be affected by the shortage, and you can share your abundant crops with other home brewers.

An important note: *Your hops vines are perennials, and they will need up to four years to be fully established and produce a full harvest of hop flowers. Your first year may seem barren. Do not give up. The second year will produce a much lusher vine and lots of foliage, but few flowers to harvest. By the third year, you can expect to see a good number of flower clusters. Keep your main vines trained to the support strings, and remove the excess shoots. By pruning in this way, the energy of the plant will go into your primary vines and promote better flower-cluster growth that can give you an abundant harvest.*

Toward the end of the growing season, you will notice that the buds are beginning to dry out slightly. They will be dry to the touch and a bit pale in color. This is the time to pick your flower buds, or cones. Take down the vines or trellis system, lay your vines flat on the ground, and unwrap the vines carefully from the guy wires. Gently hold the cone in your hand, and pull it off. If you are unable to take the vines down, then pick your cones using a ladder; although this method is not as easy.

The harvested cones should be air-dried before storing. Cones can be dried on large screens that allow for maximum air movement and prevent mold or mildew from setting in before they are completely dry. Old screens from windows or screen doors work beautifully for the drying process; they can also be made using netting or mesh stapled to a wooden frame.

You can use a food dehydrator for drying your hops. Set the unit on 95 degrees Fahrenheit (35 degrees Celsius) and dry them according to your unit's instructions. It can take you a number of runs if you have a full harvest; so prepare ahead.

To best store your dried cones, freeze them; this will lock in the aromatic oils that flavor your beers. Place your dried cones in zip-seal or vacuum-seal freezer bags. When they are stored this way, it is easy to take out the amount you want any time you need them for a batch of beer.

At the end of the season, you can bury healthy bottom vines to grow new plants the next spring. Simply bury the vines in a shallow trench and mark their location. In spring, dig them up and cut them into pieces about 4 inches long, making sure each new cutting has an eye or bud.

After harvesting, your hops vines must be cut back before winter. Prune them to a 3- or 4-inch base just above ground level. Each plant mound will then need to be covered with 8 to 10 inches of pine, straw, or wood-chip mulch. The vines will lie dormant throughout the winter months. In early spring, give each plant mound a feeding of balanced fertilizer to start out its growth spurt and begin the growing cycle again.

Take thorough notes each year, and learn from your mistakes. If your trellis did not hold, use the winter to improve on your structural plan. If you had too many June bugs this year, do some research on how you can add other plants or beneficial insects to your garden. Learn how to make the necessary modifications that will help your hops grow to their best ability. Hops gardening is a year-round activity; take the time to enjoy it, and become an expert for your own hop yard.

Chapter 5

Brewing Hops

"The roots and herbes beaten and put into new ale or beer and daily drunk, cleareth, strengtheneth, and quickeneth the sight of the eyes."
— *Nicholas Culpeper, English physician*

Different herbs are used in order to produce different flavors and bitterness in beer. *Lists of these herbs, as well as information on how to grow and dry them in preparation for adding them to the beer during fermentation, are included in this chapter.* There will be information about where to plant the herbs and how to care for them, including disease and pest control.

"The most common herbs my customers plant and use for brewing are chamomile, mint, lemon balm, and yarrow."
— *Annette Pelliccio, founder & CEO, The Happy Gardener, Inc.*

Herb name	Scientific name	Other names	Hardiness zone	Visual description	How to grow	How to harvest
Alecost	Chrysanthemum balsamita	Costmary, bible leaf	4 to 8	Bitter perennial with serrated leaves and yellow flowers	Plant in full sun.	Pick leaves regularly.
Anise hyssop	Agastache foeniculum	Giant blue hyssop, licorice mint	5 and up	Tall plant in the mint family; dark-green, triangular leaves and spiky, blue purple flowers	Plant in well-drained soil in full sun.	Pick leaves and flowers continually as the plant blooms
Basil	Ocimum basilicum	Sweet basil, Genovese basil	Delicate plant that does not live through a frost	Bushy plant with smooth, oval leaves and spikes of blue-white flowers	Rich soil in the full sun	Pick leaves continually, and remove flower heads as they appear to foster leaf growth.
Bee balm	Monarda didyma	Bergamot, oswego tea	4 to 8	Tall plant with round red or purple blooms	Plant in rich, wet soil that receives full sun.	Harvest should occur as soon as the plant blooms.

Herb name	Scientific name	Other names	Hardiness zone	Visual description	How to grow	How to harvest
Betony	Stachys officinalis	Woundwort, Common hedge nettle	4 to 9	Tall plant with spiky pink or red flowers	Tolerates average soil and full sun to partial shade	Harvest the leaves prior to flowering.
Birch	Betula	Sweet birch, yellow birch, black birch	4 to 7	Tree or shrub whose twigs smell of wintergreen	Plant trees in the fall after running the roots.	Cut new growth twigs or tap in early spring for birch sap to use instead of water.
Blackberry	Rubus	Brambleberry, cloudberry, dewberry, thimbleberry	4 to 8	Thorny bramble bush with fruit that grows after flowers	Sheltered site with full sun and good drainage	Pick ripe berries daily.

Herb name	Scientific name	Other names	Hardiness zone	Visual description	How to grow	How to harvest
Blessed thistle	Cnicus benedictus	Carduus, St. Benedict's thistle	Delicate plant that does not live through a frost	Spiky leaves similar to dandelion	Full sun in well-drained, loamy soil	Harvest entire plant after blooming.
Borage	Borago officinalis	Beebread, star flower	Very hardy	Bristly, oval leaves and star-shaped blue flowers that droop	Neutral soil in full sun or inside in pots	Pick new flowers and leaves throughout season.
Chamomile	Chamaemelum nobile	Roman chamomile	4 to 8	Low-growing and fernlike with small, daisy-like flowers that have an apple smell	Acidic, sandy soil and full sun	Flowers are picked as their petals turned back.

Herb name	Scientific name	Other names	Hardiness zone	Visual description	How to grow	How to harvest
Clary sage	*Salvia sclarea*	*Clary, clear eye*	4 to 9	*Fuzzy, heart-shaped leaves that are dark green; spiky flowers from white to lilac blue*	*Well-drained, average to sandy soil in the full sun*	*Pick new flowers and leaves throughout season.*
Coriander	*Coriandrum sativum*	*Cilantro, coriander seeds, Chinese parsley*	Very hardy	*Lobed, bright-green leaves; white to red flowers*	*Rich soil in the full sun*	*Pick leaves before the plant flowers.*
Dandelion	*Taraxacum officinale*	*Lionstooth, yellow gowan, Irish daisy*	2 to 9	*Simple basal leaves; yellow floret flowers*	*Sometimes regarded as weeds; prolific reseeding through parachute-like, fluffy seed clusters*	*Flowers, stems, leaves, and roots are all used for various purposes.*

Herb name	Scientific name	Other names	Hardiness zone	Visual description	How to grow	How to harvest
Elder	Sambucus nigra	Black Elder, Pie or Bore Tree	1 to 4	White fragrant flowers with juicy, purple-black berries; soft stems that can be hollowed	Grow wider than they are high from cuttings and may be planted as a hedge	Collect bark in autumn, leaves, flowers or berries while still green.
Elecampane	I. helenium	Horse-heal or Marchalan	1 to 4	3- to 5-foot stiff stems with ragged leaves and 2-inch, yellow dandelion-like flowers	Grow in shady damp, well drained, loamy soil.	Harvest roots from young plants under 2 years old.
Gentian	Gentiana L.		Very Hardy	Very long thick roots, 3- to 4-foot leafy stems, large orange-yellow flower clusters	Plant seeds in full sun, neutral to acidic well-drained soil. Grow well in rock gardens	Harvest and dry rhizome and roots in autumn.

Herb name	Scientific name	Other names	Hardiness zone	Visual description	How to grow	How to harvest
Ginger	Zingiber officinale		Grow indoors or zones 9 to 11 in the U.S.	3- to 4-foot leafy, reedy perennial with white or pink flower buds, blooming into yellow flowers	Grow from roots suspended over and submerged in water. Plant in moist potting soil when roots sprout.	Young rhizomes harvested and dried
Ginseng	Panax quinquefolius	Ginnsuu	3 to 9	9- to 18-inch plants with yellow or white/green flowers	Grows wild in the Mid and Eastern U.S.; also from seed	Grow in the shade in rich, wet soils.
Greek oregano	Origanum vulgare		1 to 4	Up to 20 inches, compact with hairy leaves and small white flowers	Grow from seed at 70° F or warmer, by division in the spring or from cuttings in summer.	Grow in sunny, rich soil.

Herb name	Scientific name	Other names	Hardiness zone	Visual description	How to grow	How to harvest
Heather	Calluna vulgaris	Scotch or Ling Heather	4 to 7	Low mound of greenery with prolific, colorful flower spikes	Full sun, well-drained acidic soil. Rock gardens provide shelter from cold.	Harvest flowers in full bloom and dry.
Horehound	Marrubium vulgare	White or common horehound	1 to 7	Resembles mint with dense hairy leaves and white flowers	Plant divisions, seeds, or cuttings in dry soil.	Harvest young green leaves and shoots.
Hyssop	Hyssopus officinalis	Garden hyssop, Yssop, Hyssop Herb, Isopo, Ysopo	3 to 11	Woody, branched stems with blue flower clusters towards the top	Plant divisions, seeds, or cuttings in full sun and dry soil.	Harvest at peak maturity on a dry day. Dry leaves for use.

Herb name	Scientific name	Other names	Hardiness zone	Visual description	How to grow	How to harvest
Juniper	Juniperus L.		3 to 9	Coniferous shrubs or trees with needle/leaves and seed cones that are berry-like	Sun to part shade in well-drained soil. Taller varieties have deeper root systems than low growing hedges.	Harvest berries when ripe.
Lavender	Lavandula angustifolia	Lavendin	4 to 8	Whorled purple flowers on spikes above long narrow leaves	Plant cuttings in full sun and loose soil with good drainage.	Cut brightly bloomed flowers at the bottom of the stems on dry days and hang to dry.

Herb name	Scientific name	Other names	Hardiness zone	Visual description	How to grow	How to harvest
Lemon balm	Melissa officinalis	Sweet balm, sweet Mary, Balm, Honey plant, cure-all, dropsy plant	4 to 9	In the mint family; 70 to 100 centimeters tall with small white flowers	Full sun to partial shade or indoors	
Licorice	Glycyrrhiza glabra	Liquorice	7 to 9	Many feather-like leaves with white to purplish flowers and seed pods	Full sun, deep fertile well-drained soil	Harvest pods in the autumn.

Herb name	Scientific name	Other names	Hardiness zone	Visual description	How to grow	How to harvest
Milk thistle	Silybum eburneum	Silver Milk Thistle, Elephant Thistle, or Ivory Thistle	5 to 9	Tall, erect stem over toothy, sharp leaves. Flower head is purplish and round.	Anywhere in sun to light shade	At the end of growing when white tuft appears, harvest flower heads for drying.
Mint	Mentha pipperita	Peppermint	3 to 11	Vigorous spreader with long branches that fall over and root. Small, soft, hairy leaves with white or pink flower spikes.	Anywhere from sun to shade. Works best in pots that contain spreading.	Green sprigs and leaves may be cut for use as needed.
Nasturtium	Tropaeolum		9 to 11	Varieties may bush, trail, or climb. Rounded, wide, dark-green leaves and brightly colored flowers	Start from seed in sun to shade.	Harvest leaves and flowers at the height of ripeness.

Herb name	Scientific name	Other names	Hardiness zone	Visual description	How to grow	How to harvest
Nettles	Urtica dioica	Stinging Nettles, burn nettle, burn weed, burn hazel	5 to 9	Soft, serrated leaves on a wiry stem. Leaves have stinging bristles.	Sun to shade in a well-watered spot	Harvest wearing gloves! Cooked or dried nettles will not sting like green growing plants do. Harvest any time.
Raspberry	Rubus Idaeus	Red or Common raspberry	3 to 8	Small, serrated leaves on long canes with small, sharp stickers. Flowers are small and white, producing bright pink to purple berries	Plant in sun in well-drained soil. Allow up to 4 feet per bush.	Pick ripe fruit, and then cut back the spent canes to the base of the bush.
Rhubarb	Rheum rhabarbarum		3 to 8	2- to 3-foot plant with leafy stalks. Stalks turn deep red when ripe.	Divide and plant in sun. Water regularly removing flowers.	Cut stalks for use at the plant. Use only stalks, not the leaves.

Herb name	Scientific name	Other names	Hardiness zone	Visual description	How to grow	How to harvest
Rosehips	Rhugosa Rose	Salt spray or Beach tornado	5 to 8	Heavy-veined and wrinkled, green foliage with large sprays of blossoms	Plant in well-drained or sandy soil in full sun.	Harvest rose hips or berries when they are large and ripe.
Rosemary	Rosmarinus officinalis		8 to 10	Long, woody stems with small, soft needle-like leaves covering the entire length	Full sun with good drainage. Allow 2 to 3 feet for growth.	Harvest new shoots for consumption and older stems for use in flavoring.
Sage	Salvia officinalis		2 to 10	Wiry stems with soft hairy flat leaves.	Full sun; well drained soil	Cut and dry healthy green leaves.
Savory	Satureja hortensis		5 to 10	Slender, tall stems with bronze leaves and small, white flower clusters	Full sun with moderate water and rich soil	Cut and dry healthy green leaves.
Spruce	Picea pungens	Colorado Spruce or Blue Spruce	3 to 8	Tall, coniferous evergreen	Plant in sun with well-drained soil and plenty of vertical room.	Cut branches in autumn for drying.

Herb name	Scientific name	Other names	Hardiness zone	Visual description	How to grow	How to harvest
Sweet woodruff	Galium odoratum		4 to 8	Dark-green, lance-shaped leaves with small, white star-shaped blooms	Plant in well-drained shade and water often.	Cut and dry healthy leafy stems.
Thyme	Thymus vulgaris	English Thyme	5 to 9	Long, branchy stems with small, folded, dark-green leaves and small, white flower clusters	Plant in sunny well-drained soil.	Cut stems for drying leaves.
Valerian	Valeriana officinalis	Garden Heliotrope, All Heal	4 to 9	Clumpy rhizome with branching stems that produce feathery leaves and rounded clusters of pink, white, or lavender flowers	Full sun to part shade in sandy loam	Harvest roots in fall for drying. Odor can be offensive and pungent.
Winter-green	Gaultheria procumbens		3 to 7	Long, creeping stems with leathery, oval, dark-green leaves. Berries and flowers may occur and hang on from season to season.	Plant in shady well-drained soil and water well frequently.	Harvest green leaves for flavoring and medicinal usage.

Herb name	Scientific name	Other names	Hardiness zone	Visual description	How to grow	How to harvest
Yarrow	Achillea millefolium	Thousand-leaf, gordoloba, thousand-leaf clover, green arrow, nosebleed, dog daisy, bloodwort, cammack and old-mans pepper	3 to 8	Fern-like, aromatic leaves with flat flower clusters	Plant in full sun in well-drained soil.	Harvest green leaves for drying.

CASE STUDY: ANNETTE PELLICIO

Founder & CEO
The Happy Gardener, Inc.
804-798-9280
www.thehappygardener.info

I only use organics in my herb garden. It is important to use non-toxic products when growing edibles. Planting certain herbs together will discourage pesky insects from feeding on your plants. For example, planting lavender and chives next to each other will keep aphids and caterpillars away. I also use Happy Naturals brand of organic foliar feeds on herbs. The Outdoor Foliar Feed is applied to the herb leaves and stems once a month to feed, increase growth, and control pests. It is made from 100-percent vegetable-based oils and sea vegetables, so it is safe to use up until the day of harvest.

The peace I experience when working in the soil and watching everything grow and bloom. I have an extensive herb and vegetable garden, and I love being able to use my edibles to make our meals, knowing they are made from the most nutritious and toxin-free ingredients.

I usually grow basil, parsley, chives, oregano, cilantro, rosemary, watermelon, cantaloupe, eggplant, tomatoes, lettuce, cucumber, zucchini, corn, Brussels sprouts, and tons of roses. I begin planting my herbs from seeds in early spring. I use organic pest control Outdoor Foliar Feed from my company, The Happy Gardener. In order to control pests, I use organic Pre-emergent Weed Control, which is also available from The Happy Gardener, and I apply it in early spring and throughout the summer in beds.

I grow all of my herbs in containers. However, I have worked with home brewers who use garden areas for their herbs for larger quantity. Starting your herbs from seed does best and is the least expensive and easiest way to grow. Fill a pot with potting soil and scatter the seeds on top, cover with ¼-inch soil, and water using a spray bottle so not to drown. Herb seedlings will emerge in about seven days. Keep soil moist. Insects and enough sun exposure is the biggest challenge with growing herbs. Herbs grow best in exposures with four to six hours of full sun.

Your herbs are ready to harvest once they have established enough leaves and before they start to flower. Late summer is the best time to harvest. To dry the herbs, cut the branches and remove any dry or dying leaves. Remove the lower leaves to expose branches, bundle four to six branches together, and tie as a bunch. Punch out several holes in a paper bag. Label the bag with the name of the herb. Place the herb bundle upside down in the bag. Gather the ends of the bag around the bundle and tie closed. Hang the bundle upside down in a warm room. Drying will take about two to three weeks. You can store dried herbs in an airtight container for up to a year. Or you can freeze them in freezer bags for up to six months.

I work in my garden everyday. I am a third-generation, gardening business owner, so I grew up with it. While I do not use my herbs in creating home brew, I have a couple of customers who do. Our company manufactures our exclusive line of organic products for plant foods, weed control, pest control, and more.

Chapter 6

Culture Your
Own Yeast

"I feel sorry for people who don't drink. When they wake up in the morning, that's as good as they're going to feel all day."
— *Frank Sinatra*

This chapter takes you from the garden to a home laboratory. Even if you were not great at biology or chemistry in school, culturing your own yeast is not that difficult and can save you money, because you will be growing yeast in your home rather than having to buy a culture every time you brew.

Yeast is a one-celled fungus. Even before our ancestors knew what yeast was, they were able to produce beer because yeast is everywhere in nature. Brewing with wild yeast can have unpredictable results, as bad yeasts or bacteria often spoil these brews.

Louis Pasteur, noted scientist, finally discovered yeasts and was able to isolate different species and strains. In doing this, he proved that fermentation was not spontaneous; rather, it could be controlled. In the 19th century, Emil Hansen applied the work of Pasteur to brewing.

Basically, only two species of yeasts used in brewing. These yeasts are in the Saccharomyces genus and have been domesticated for use specifically in brewing. The ale yeast is S. cervisiae, and the lager yeast is S. uvarum. These yeasts exist in an oxygen-deprived, or anaerobic, environment, so they survive and multiply by digesting and converting sugars into alcohol and carbon dioxide. In addition to these two main by-products, about 500 other compounds are produced by yeast. These other compounds contribute to the taste of the finished beer.

In Appendix C, there is a list of a number of strains of these two main yeasts. These strains, along with the hops, herbs, and grain, are what create distinctively different beers. The different strains also contribute to different rates of flocculation, attenuation, and fermentation temperature ranges. Flocculation is the yeast coming together in clumps to create a sort of crust on the top of a fermenting beer. Attenuation is the degree to which yeast is able to ferment the sugars in beer. *These two terms will be explored in detail in Appendix C.*

Beginning to Culture

In order to get the desired results from yeast in a beer, you must choose the right type of yeast — and, more importantly, the correct strain of yeast. You can create a number of different styles of beer from one strain of yeast.

In order to properly culture yeast at home, you must do so under sterile conditions. Sterile means that the area you are working in must be completely free of microbial life. You can purchase yeast culture kits that contain all of the sterile equipment needed to do the culturing. You just need to make sure that the area you will be working in is as sterile a condition as possible. *You will learn more about how to prepare that area later in the chapter.*

You can buy a yeast culturing kit from a home-brew store like Midwest Supplies. *See their contact information in Appendix B.*

Here is what their kit contains (each of these items will be explained in the instructions below):

- 50-milliliter flask or 10-milliliter vial (these can be used interchangeably)
- #2 solid stopper
- Alcohol lamp
- 8 disposable sterile loops
- 3 pre-filled malt-agar medium plates
- 1 slant tube
- Malt extract for 1-liter yeast starter

They also recommend that you also have the following on-hand:

- Pure liquid yeast culture
- Extra agar for creating slant tubes (these can be purchased at local Asian or specialty food markets)
- 1000-milliliter flask (Sometimes referred to as a Erlenmeyer flask, it is cone-shaped with a neck so it is easier to hold the flask and put a stopper in it.)
- Stopper and air lock

- Malt nutrient

- A pressure cooker for sterilizing equipment

Before you begin, you need to plan. Yeast culturing should be done in advance of using the yeast to ferment a beer. You need to give the yeast enough time to build up in their numbers to be able to handle a 5-gallon bucket of wort.

Here is a typical five-day breakdown of how to prepare a yeast culture for fermentation:

- Day 1: Inoculate the 10-milliliter starter from plate or slant. Inoculate means placing the live yeasts on a media in order for them to grow. Plates and slants are media that provide yeasts with the nutrients they need in order to grow and multiply. A plate is sometimes referred to as a Petri dish. A Petri dish is a thin, round container that contains malt agar, which is food for yeast. You can use a plate to determine whether a culture is a pure strain or whether it has been contaminated. If it has been contaminated, it must be thrown out, and you must start over. A slant also contains wort-agar, but the surface is slanted, which promotes oxygen exposure. Slants can be refrigerated for long-term storage for up to a year. The 10-milliliter starter is a malt extract solution that has been prepared. The yeast from the media is added to the starter in preparation of being added to the wort.

- Day 2: The yeast begins to grow in the starter. The starter must be placed in a place that is at least 70 degrees Fahrenheit.

- Day 3: The yeast starter continues to grow. The 10-milliliter starter is added to a larger 1000-milliliter flask to encourage even more growth and more food for the yeast. The 1000-milliliter flask is filled with more liquid malt extract.

- Day 4: The yeast will continue to grow, and you will see bubbling, which is the sign that fermentation is beginning in the starter.

- Day 5: The yeast is pitched into the wort in order for the process of fermentation to begin and convert the wort into beer.

This schedule works well for creating a 5-gallon batch of beer. Each step only takes a few minutes to accomplish on each of the days. If you start with a good culture, you will not need to do anything to get it started.

Creating a Culture

This next section is a systematic process of creating the slant or plate to be used in preparing a yeast culture.

Step 1: Site preparation

You can set up your lab anywhere, but it should be in a place that is free from possible contaminants. This means that it should not be around any drafts caused by fans, open windows, or air conditioning vents. In addition, the surface you are working on needs to be sanitary. You need to clean the table or counter top so well you can eat off of it. It needs to be clutter-free, and you need plenty of space to work on. You can wipe the area with any cleaner that says that it is antiviral and antibacterial.

The greatest risk of contamination will come from airborne bacteria. This is why a draft or wind should be avoided as bacteria can blow in and land on your clean area. After you have wiped the area clean, light your alcohol lamp, and place it in the center of your working area. You may want to invest in some latex gloves and face masks. You can buy these from most pharmacies; this will reduce the amount of contamination that you could unwillingly supply.

Step 2: Flaming

This is the next stage in keeping your materials sterile. The flame will not only keep microbes from landing in your space, but also will kill microbes on contact. Flaming is the process of passing equipment through the flame. You need to be very careful doing this so that you do not burn your hands or start a fire; it is always a good idea to have a fire extinguisher on hand whenever you are working with fire. You do not need to hold the vials or equipment in the flame. You need only pass them slowly through the flame a few times.

Flaming should be done whenever you open or close a container. You should pass the lip of the container and the cap through the flame. The glass of the flask and tubes are Pyrex® glass, which means they are flame resistant. Remember that plastic and rubber will melt and catch fire, so only pass them through the flame.

Step 3: Using plates and slants

Once you have flamed your equipment, it is time to create the cultures. Using a plate is one of the best ways to create a culture that you can then make a starter yeast from. It not only allows your yeast to grow, but you can also see the purity of your culture and determine if there are any contaminants. You will be able to see another colony growing that is different than the one you added to the plate.

Molds

Molds are the most common type of contaminants. They look like the type of mold you might see on cheese, fruit, or bread.

Bacteria

Bacteria may be a little harder to identify, because they can look similar to yeast. The difference is that bacteria will be either translucent or colored, whereas brewer's yeast is creamy and opaque.

Yeast

You can identify your yeast growing as it will grow in a globe shape, or you may see it in single colonies that will look like creamy disks with peak-like centers. Once you inoculate the disk, there are millions of yeast cells, so you will need only a small amount to create a yeast starter.

If you find that there are bacteria or molds growing, you will need to discard the disk and start over.

You will be creating plates from your slant, or mother culture. If a plate is contaminated, move more yeast from your slant onto a new plate. You can store a slant in the refrigerator for a year; a plate will last only a couple of months. You want to keep your slant pure, so that you can reuse it. A plate you will only use once.

If you find that your slant is contaminated, you will need to create a new one.

Creating a Slant

A slant is a glass test tube with agar-wort media in the bottom. The media is a solid gel-like substance, and while it was solidifying, it was held at a slant; therefore, the media is in a solid, slanted shape in the bottom of the tube.

Each slant is a mother culture and will contain one strain of yeast. You can have many different slants with different strains of yeast, or you may even have backup slants for a particular strain of yeast in case one becomes contaminated. You will need a pure yeast culture to work with.

With your loop, scoop a pinprick amount of pure yeast, and drop it onto the media of the slant. Use the loop to spread the yeast over the entire surface of the slant. Once it is smeared, use the flame to sterilize the cap and lip of the tube, and fasten the cap loosely on top. You will have an adequate-sized colony in about two days. Make sure that the slant is kept in controlled temperature of about 70 degrees Fahrenheit during that period. You have now created a master slant.

You can create backup slants from this original master slant. To create a backup slant, you will need to use your loop to transfer from one slant to another. *Here is a simplified process of transferring:*

1. Use a rack (which you can buy at the same place you bought your yeast culture kit), and place the master slant and backup slants ready to go.

2. Loosen the caps on both slants.

3. Open the master slant and flame the rim and cap. Use a loop and pick out a small amount of yeast. Replace the cap and place the master slant on the rack.

4. Open the backup slant and flame the rim and cap. Deposit and smear the yeast in the backup slant.

5. Recap the backup slant loosely, and allow the yeast to grow. Like the master slant, it needs a temperature of about 70 degrees Fahrenheit.

6. Place the master slant back in the refrigerator right away. After the two days have passed, you can see the white yeast colony in the backup slant; tighten the cap, and place it in the refrigerator as well.

Choosing the Right Colony

A healthy yeast colony will be a creamy white color. A slant usually has one slick yeast colony, whereas a plate may have a number of colonies dotting the surface. Even though there may be a number of different dots and groups of colonies on a plate, you should choose a single colony dot. These are purest colonies and the most likely to do well in a starter. All you need to do is select one of these colonies, scoop it with a sterile loop, and place it into a 10-millileter starter. Once the colony is in the starter, seal the top, and it is ready to start growing. Here is the process of making a starter from a plate:

1. Clean the area you are working in, and sterilize it as much as possible. Light your alcohol burner.

2. Put the plate upside down on the counter.

3. Loosen the cap on the 10-millileter vial.

4. Turn the plate over, near the flame. Use the loop and scrape up the colony you wish to use.

5. Turn the plate back upside down.

6. Flame the lip of the vial.

7. Dunk the yeast on the end of the loop into the starter.

8. Flame the lip of the vial again.

9. Screw the cap on tightly and then slightly loosen it. This loosening allows gas to escape, which promotes healthy growth of the yeast.

10. Shake the starter slightly and mix the yeast into the malt suspension.

Over the next 24 to 48 hours, the yeast will grow in the starter. Remember to keep the temperature at 70 degrees Fahrenheit. You will see sediment form on the bottom of the starter vial. This white sediment is yeast; it is normal and a good sign that it is growing.

Yeast Starter Ready for Pitching

Once the two days have passed, it is time to either refrigerate the yeast or move to the next step. The yeast on the slant will keep for seven days in the refrigerator. You need to make sure that it is once again room temperature when you are ready to transfer it to the Erlenmeyer flask.

Step 1

You will need to sanitize the Erlenmeyer flask, a glass triangle-shaped beaker. This can be done two ways. The first is to use a sanitizer, such as B-Brite™, that you would normally use for cleaning beer equipment. Fill the flask with water and a couple of tablespoons of sanitizer. Allow it to soak 15 minutes, rinse with hot water, and drain. Cap the top with aluminum foil. You are then ready to move to Step 2.

The second method is more preferred; this is the baking method. Place foil on top of the flask and mold it tight around the lip. Place the flask in a 350-degree, preheated oven for two hours. Allow it to cool before proceeding to Step 2.

Step 2

Boil 400 millileters of water. Add 4 tablespoons of malt nutrient to the water and add the mixture to the Erlenmeyer flask.

Step 3

Tighten the cap on the vial. Shake the culture to mix the yeast into the solution.

Step 4

Loosen the cap and flame with alcohol burner around the lip.

Step 5

Quickly flame the lip of the flask.

Step 6

Pour liquid from the vial into the flask and quickly cover with foil.

Step 7

While holding the foil tightly on the top, gently shake the flask to mix the yeast with the nutrient.

Step 8

Allow the flask to sit for one to two days before pitching into beer wort.

Step 9

When you are ready to pitch into wort, remove the foil and flame the flask lip. If you are using a plastic fermenter, you can pitch directly into wort; if you are using a glass carboy, you will want to flame the rim of the carboy.

Step 10

Cover the fermenter with a lid — or a stopper, in the case of a carboy. Gently rock the wort to mix the yeast and the wort.

Step 11

You will begin to see signs of fermentation in the form of foam or bubbles within six to 24 hours. For ale, keep the temperature range between 55 to 70 degrees Fahrenheit; for lager, keep the temperature between 48 and 55 degrees Fahrenheit.

Find a Colony by Streaking

You can find the right colony to use for your plate through a process called **streaking**. This process is an easy way to isolate yeast colonies and make sure of their purity. The process is done by taking the inoculation loop and streaking it across the agar surface in patterns of decreasing numbers of cells. These last cells will be wide apart and will grow into single isolated colonies. Here is the process of streaking a plate:

Step 1

Clean your area and light the alcohol lamp.

Step 2

Place the plate you are working with closer to the lamp with the agar side facing down.

Step 3

Take the slant you are working with, and after removing the cap, flame the rim.

Step 4

Dip your inoculation tip — the end with the little loop — into the yeast in the slant, and scoop out a small sample. Quickly re-flame the rim, and close the slant with the cap.

Step 5

Flip over the plate, and hold near the flame. Take the loop, and run in a few times on one section. Streak the loop through this section by running it in one direction like you are painting through the yeast sample. Chose another section, and streak it through this new section. Repeat the streaking a few more times on different sections of the plate. When done, cover the plate with Parafilm®. Parafilm® is a unique, self-sealing, moldable, and flexible film that you can use to cover your plate.

Step 6

Grow the colonies on the plate for three days. Make sure the temperature is about 70 degrees Fahrenheit. You will see the growth when your streak is dense with yeast. In later streaks on the surface, the colonies will be less dense. If done correctly, you should be able to locate isolated colonies.

Step 7

After the three days of growth, make sure the plate is still covered with Parafilm®, and place the plate in the refrigerator. You are now ready to use the plate to create a yeast starter.

Helpful Tips

Here are a number of tips for culturing your own yeast for brewing beer at home:

1. Make sure that when you are transferring yeast cells from one container to the next that you flame the rim of both containers before and after the transfer. This reduces the risk of contamination.

2. Before you begin to transfer a yeast solution, you need to swirl it in order to make sure that the yeast has not settled on the bottom and that it is distributed in the solution.

3. If your yeast is in a solution, you need to shake the solution to ensure that it is well aerated. Your yeast needs oxygen to grow.

4. Never freeze your plates or slants. Always place them in a refrigerator for storage. Cold slows the growth down and preserves your yeast, while freezing them will kill your culture.

5. Between uses, it is recommended that you wrap your plates with Parafilm®. This will prevent contamination and drying out.

6. When you are streaking or transferring your yeast culture from one container to another, be sure to work as close to your alcohol flame as possible. This will prevent contamination by other microbes.

7. During a transfer of yeast from one container to another, be sure that you perform this process quickly, and flame and close your containers. This will prevent possible contamination.

8. Be sure to label all your slants and plates with the name of the culture and the date they were created.

9. Read this chapter on culturing and the step-by-step instructions before opening your containers to remind you of what you need to do, because you can ruin cultures through hesitation and simple mistakes.

Sterilization of Equipment

In order to reuse equipment for yeast culturing, it is not enough to just use bleach or sanitizer. It must be pressure sanitized. In labs and hospitals, they do this with an instrument called an **autoclave**. This piece of technology costs tens of thousands of dollars and is not practical for home use. You can use a pressure cooker to get the same level of sterilization.

An autoclave works by placing the instruments inside. Steam is forced in the autoclave, and vents are opened so that all the air is removed. The exhaust vents are then closed. Pressure from the steam will rise to about 15 pounds per square inch and is held there for 10 minutes or more. At that temperature and pressure, all the organisms in the chamber and on that equipment are killed.

A pressure cooker can be used in much the same way. One of the first things you should do before attempting to sterilize equipment is read the safety instructions, and even call the manufacturer about safety issues using the pressure cooker. Pressure cookers can be dangerous and can even explode if not used correctly. This is a rare occurrence, but safety needs to be of primary concern.

Make sure all the valves and seals are undamaged and are in good working order. You can buy replacements at hardware stores or from the pressure cooker manufacturer. If you have an older model, pressure cooker seals may not be available, and you may need to purchase a new pressure cooker. Pressure cookers can be bought at most kitchen supply stores or can be found online at sites like Amazon.com. Presto and Mirro brands are good choices. Prices range from $75 to $100. You should buy at least a 6-quart or larger size. You need to make sure that you buy a model with a steam pressure gauge.

Here are some other safety tips when using a pressure cooker:

- Do not over-tighten the lid. You can turn the lid clockwise until it stops, and then loosen about a ⅜-turn.

- Allow items to cool prior to moving them from the pressure cooker. Be careful when touching the glasses because sometimes they break under the pressure.

- Do not try to sterilize plates unless they are made of glass. Plastic ones will melt during the process of autoclaving.

Here are step-by-step instructions for sterilizing your yeast culturing equipment using a pressure cooker:

Step 1

Place items in the pressure cooker one deep. Do not stack items. However, do not place any of the items directly on the bottom of the cooker; you should use the rack supplied with the cooker.

Step 2

Once you have loaded the pressure cooker, you will add the amount of water that your particular pressure cooker's set of instructions tell you to use. For a 6-quart cooker, you would use about 3 cups of water. You should never leave a pressure cooker alone, and if you start seeing signs that the water has boiled out — like steam stops escaping through the valve, you may need to add more water.

Step 3

Turn on the heat with the exhaust valves open. Air inside the pressure cooker can escape.

Step 4

Once you see steam being released through the valve, close the exhaust valve. You have to make sure all the air in the cooker is removed or the temperature inside the cooker will not reach the level necessary to sterilize your equipment.

Step 5

You will begin sterilization time after the pressure reaches 15 pounds. If you are sterilizing using a 6- to 8-quart pressure cooker, your sterilization time should be 15 minutes. If you are using upwards to a 20-quart cooker, your sterilization time should be 30 minutes, and if it is above 20 quarts, your sterilization time should be 60 minutes.

You might let the cooker cool overnight. Do not open the cooker during this period. When you do open the cooker, before you remove the slants, you should screw the caps on them to ensure that they remain sterile.

Storing your Sterilized Items

Remember that microbes from the air can fall on your equipment; so it is important that you properly store sterilized items. If you were working in a professional lab, you might have what they call a "dust-free" box. This special box keeps sterile items sterile. You can create your own dust-free box out of cardboard or plastic milk cartons.

Cardboard milk cartons

You will need two cardboard milk cartons. Clean both boxes well after they are empty. Rinse them with scalding hot water until you are sure that they no longer contain any milk. Place them upside down, and let them dry before using. You can create a dust-free box by cutting all the way around the top of the straight sides below the triangular part of the carton. Pinch, and then cut each of the four corners left at the top about a half-inch down. This will create a V-shaped cutout at each corner. Set the first carton aside.

Take the other carton and cut around the box 60 millimeters above the bottom. You can then turn this lid upside down, and let it telescope over the box made from the first carton.

Plastic milk jug

You can also make a dust-free box from two plastic quart milk cartons. Be sure to clean each out, and make sure they are clean of any milk. You use the same technique as mentioned above. You may want to create the lid first and trim away on the other jug until you create the dust-free box. You can then place sterilized items inside these dust-free boxes. Pull the lid off, take out what you need, and then replace the lid quickly.

Yeast from Beer

Once you have mastered the process of creating cultures from pure yeast sources, you can try your hand at creating cultures from beer bottles. These techniques will not work for all beers because some use different mixes of yeasts that would make it impossible to culture, and you must use beer that has some sediment to work with.

You can test whether sediment will work by streaking some of the sediment on a plate. If you cannot find individual colonies within a few days, then the sample may not work as base yeast. *It may not work as a culture, but you can try to use the sediment directly in a 10-millileter starter, as mentioned earlier.*

Some beers, like Hefeweizen, may not work for a yeast starter, because many of these beers have had the ale yeast removed during the process of fermentation and replaced with lager yeast. Sierra Nevada brand beer works well as an ale yeast culture.

Here is the process of extracting yeast from a beer:

Step 1

Set up your area with your alcohol lamp burning and a 10-millileter vial ready. Uncap a fresh beer — not one you just drank. Pour the beer into a glass to drink later. Leave a tablespoon of beer left in the bottom. You should be able to see sediment in the bottom of the bottle.

Step 2

Swirl the leftover beer and yeast until it is dissolved into the beer.

Step 3

Flame the opening of the bottle, and cap and flame the 10-millileter container.

Step 4

Pour in a little bit of the beer into the vial. Re-flame and cap the vial.

Step 5

Aerate the sample by shaking the vial. Loosen the cap slightly to allow gas to escape.

Step 6

Leave for three days in a temperature of about 70 degrees Fahrenheit.

Step 7

You may choose to pitch into a starter for a beer ready to be fermented. You also have the choice of using a loop and streaking a plate. You will need to gather the yeast from the bottom of the sample to streak the plate. If you have a good colony grown, you can cover it with Parafilm®, and refrigerate.

Now that you know how to grow all the grain, herbs, hops, and even the yeast, you are ready to learn how to put these components together to create a home brew. Even if you are a veteran of home brewing, you may want to look over the next couple of chapters. You may be surprised to learn new techniques.

Chapter 7

The Essentials of Home Brewing

"He was a wise man, who invented beer."
— *Plato, ancient Greek philosopher (427-347 BC)*

Making beer at home is legal, and an individual can produce 100 gallons of beer per year without taxation. President Jimmy Carter signed a bill in into law 1979 that allowed home brewers to make beer at home.

The exciting part about making beer at home is that it is delicious and rather easy to make. Once you grasp an understanding of how grains, hops, and yeast interact together, you will realize that thousands of different combinations of the ingredients can be used to make beer.

CASE STUDY: CIDER IS AN-OTHER TASTY OPTION FOR HOME BREWING

Lawrence Shatkin
Long-time Home brewer
Titusville, N.J.

I have been home brewing for about 15 years, but have been gardening for about 30. My wife bought me the basic supplies from a home-brew supply store because she thought it would be a hobby I would enjoy. She was right.

I do only kit brewing, but I am interested in trying specialty grains. I grow raspberries and use them to make a raspberry wheat beer, with excellent results. I use about 3 pounds of berries for 5 gallons of wort. I also make pumpkin ale, which includes real pumpkin, plus pumpkin pie spice mix.

I have a 400-square-foot garden, and I use leaves from autumn in my berry garden, where they can slowly compost over the year and add nutrients to the soil. I also have a cylindrical compost bin outdoors and put all my vegetable scraps and eggshells in there. I grow raspberries, rhubarb, tomatoes, and peppers.

I have created many different favorite beers. Right now, however, I would have to say my favorite is my coffee stout. I buy my supplies from Princeton Homebrew in Trenton, N.J. (*Information is in Appendix B*). While not traditionally a beer, ciders are made in much the same way beer and wine are, so I wanted to include my favorite recipe for home-made summer cider.

Apple Juice Cider

This is ridiculously inexpensive, yet reasonably tasty. It produces a tangy drink, good for hot summer days and with a rather strong kick. Another advantage is that supermarket juice is sterile when it comes out of the bottle, so only the added honey needs to be boiled. It is extremely important to allow the bottled brew to age because it tastes very rough when it is new.

Ingredients

5 gal. supermarket apple juice (must have no preservatives)

1 c. honey

Cider yeast. Wine yeast is also acceptable.

¾ c. priming sugar

Instructions

1. Add honey to ½ gallon cider, boil 20 minutes.

2. Add this to the remaining 4 ½ gallons in the brew bucket, pitch yeast at once (because it will already be cool enough).

3. Allow to ferment until bubbling activity ceases.

4. Boil priming sugar in 2 cups of water for 15 minutes; stir gently into brew.

5. Bottle.

6. Allow to age in bottles for at least six months; nine is even better.

The process of beer making is a relatively easy, but it is one that takes time in the beginning because you need to cook the wort and mix the grains, hops, and herbs to give it the proper flavor, aroma, and sugars for yeast to transform into beer.

To make most beers, you only need four things: water, some sort of sugar (in the form of grain), a bittering agent (usually in the form of hops and or herbs), and yeast. The process goes something like this:

Water is the essential building block of life. It is essential because yeast needs it in order to thrive. Water is also the universal solvent, so it provides a medium for the yeast to have access to the sugar that is dissolved within the liquid.

Yeast loves sugar and uses it for most of its biological functions; it eats, grows, procreates, and dies. It is the biological process of living yeast that transforms sugar into alcohol. Some lengthy biological and chemical reactions occur, but knowing the basic process is sufficient for creating world-class beer. *In Chapter 2, you learned about the sugars grains contain and how to transform the starches in grain into simple sugars that yeast love.*

Yeast consumes sugar because it is essential to its metabolic processes. Yeast metabolism is not that different from the human digestion process. When we digest food, we also transform it into a different form, whether it is gas, liquid, or solid. Energy is drawn from the sugar we eat, and what the body does not need is excreted. In the case of yeast, it is alcohol and gas. The gas is in the form of little tiny bubbles — those same bubbles you find in beer — and is composed of carbon dioxide, the same gas that humans expel when breathing.

Once the beer reaches a certain level of alcohol, the yeast will die, and the process of fermentation will cease. In some cases, not all the yeast dies, but is instead in a state of suspended animation. You have seen this state if you have ever opened a packet of yeast to make bread. It is dried and visually lifeless until water is added to it. Some beer yeast comes in the same kinds of packets as bread yeast does.

Tip: *Never use bread yeast to make beer. You will regret the decision and will quickly pour the horrible yeasty liquid bread down the drain. Bread yeast will leave a bad aftertaste in your beer, and it may not ferment at all. It is great at leavening bread, but it is not so great*

at creating alcohol. Stick to the two basic yeast types mentioned in
Chapter 6 — Ale and Yeast.

If the temperature of the beer rises or sugar is added, this yeast
can come back to life. For a home brewer, this is akin to making
liquid hand grenades. The bottles will literally explode and re-
decorate part of your house all the way to the ceiling.

Tips are provided throughout this book on how to avoid this, although if you make beer for long enough, this will probably happen at least once. Just be prepared, and do not place your bottled
beer next to any nice furniture.

If you combine the four essential ingredients, you can create just
about any kind of beer. You cannot use artificial sweeteners to
create beer, which is why you will never find sugar-free or diet
beer. Light beer is just beer with less residual sugar, that is, sugar
that is left in beer after the yeast have all died off during fermentation.

Different chemicals can be added to stop fermentation and make
beer clearer or more stable. These do not add much to the taste of
the beer, but are essential to certain chemical processes necessary
for creating a clear and clean-tasting beer.

It is the manipulation of the four essential ingredients — water,
grains, hops, and yeast — that make each beer unique and different. Let us look at each of these ingredients in more detail, as they
are the basis of creating any beer.

Water

Water is essential to all life, and it is also essential to the life of your beer. Different regions around the world create a one-of-a-kind taste in their wine, beer, and liquor just because of the water they use. You may not think that water has an actual taste, but it does. Trace minerals affect the taste, and they are also important for a healthy fermentation.

Not all water is created the same. There are a number of different sources for water:

- tap water
- spring water
- well water
- distilled water
- bottled drinking water

The next sections will detail the different types of water in terms of brewing beer.

Tap water

Where you live determines the source of your tap water. There is a wide range of tap water; just like Goldilocks, you must find the one that is just right.

This water is too hard

Hard water is full of minerals, such as calcium, magnesium, and other metals. This type of water leaves deposits on pipes and spots on dishes and kitchen utensils. You can do a simple test to determine if your water is hard. Add some water to soap. Hard water will not create or maintain foam very easily. Generally, the pH of hard water is alkaline; this can leave a bitter taste in the water, and in your beer. If you consider softening your water with a water treatment system, you should be aware that this would make the beer taste salty and unpleasant.

   Tip: *Do not use softened water to make beer.*

You should avoid using hard water, and move on to other water choices. However, soft water is not necessarily the answer. Besides being salty, the process of softening water will remove essential minerals needed for a healthy fermentation.

This water is too soft

On the other end of the spectrum is soft water, which contains fewer minerals. If you must use tap water, you want to make sure it is soft tap water. A good way to test if you have soft water is to turn it on, and place some soft soap in your hand. Rub your hands under the water; if you can create a decent lather, this is a good sign that the water is soft. Soft water is not perfect; it tends to be more acidic and leaks metals into your beer. This can give your beer a metallic or sour taste. Taste your water first, and determine if these characteristics exist before destroying a potentially good beer.

This water is just right

Relatively pH-neutral water with sufficient minerals is a good choice. You can test your water's pH at home using a water-testing kit. You can buy water-testing kits at **www.air-n-water.com**, or you can send water off to be tested at a county, state, or private lab. You can also call your county's environmental agency for suggestions.

Some water supplies have a high amount of chlorine or have been fluoridated. This can cause the taste of your beer to be off-mark. A brief boiling of your water can help release these gases without losing minerals in your water, but be careful not to over-boil it. You can also pass your water through an activated charcoal filter.

Spring water

Many homes in rural areas use spring water for their drinking water. This is the best water you can use because it contains everything you want as far as minerals, but does not contain any added chemicals, such as chlorine. If you buy spring water from a store, make sure it is really spring water and not tap water. Look at the label to confirm that it is ozonized and that it is not from a municipal water supply. Tap water from another city is not bad, but it is not really spring water. The fact that it is ozonized means no chemicals were used to kill bacteria in the water.

Well water

Well water is different from spring water because it often contains iron and other metals. *This makes it hard water, as described above.* You can try to pass it through an activated charcoal filter, but there still may be some disagreeable flavors that would not make a good choice for beer.

Distilled water

Distilled water is sometimes referred to as "dead water." All the water's living components and minerals are removed during the distillation process. Yeast cannot survive and populate in this kind of environment, so avoid using this type of processed water.

Bottled water

Many designer bottled water brands contain minerals and additives, such as salt, in an attempt to make their water more palatable. You should avoid this kind of water. Some brands do not contain a lot of additives. The grocery store brand spring water will work just fine.

> **Tip:** *Never use flavored waters or fitness water. It would not taste good at all, and it is not very likely you will get yeast to live in it.*

Yeast

Home brewing is an organic, living process rather than a set of chemical reactions that can be reproduced in a chemistry lab. Chemical reactions happen within the yeast cells, but it is a digestive process that cannot occur simply by mixing together chemicals. There is no way around it; you need live yeast cells to create any fermented product. *In Chapter 6, you learned how you can culture your own yeast. For most first-time home brewers, you can buy yeast from home-brew supply stores like those listed in Appendix B.*

212 The Complete Guide to Growing Hops, Malts, and Brewing Herbs

Like water and sugar, there are different types of yeast. You should not use bread yeast, the kind used to leaven bread. It will make your beer taste more like liquid bread.

> **Tip:** *Some brew houses have been making beer for centuries. Every nook, cranny, wall, floorboard, and implement in these structures contains particular strains of yeast; so open vat fermentation is much easier to accomplish. The beers produced in these unique structures cannot be duplicated elsewhere because the yeast strains only exist in these places.*

These little microscopic creatures live to do one thing: eat. The only food on their menu is sugar. They sometimes come freeze-dried in a small packet, especially in pre-made beer kits. When the must is ready, the packet is emptied into the wort. The water reconstitutes them, and they are ready to eat. Within a few hours ,they will eat, release gas, produce alcohol, and procreate. The next generation will begin to do the same as the parent yeast die. This dead yeast sinks to the bottom of the bucket, and when you make beer for the first time, you will see this primordial ooze. This is why you rack, or take the clear beer off the dead yeast, called trub. As you are drinking a nice Amber Bock, you taste yeast. They make up the complexity to beer and actually add some protein. Picking the right yeast strain does matter.

In the last chapter, you learned there are two basic yeast types: ale and lager. There are many different strains of yeast to choose from; a list of the most common types appears in Appendix C.

Besides dry yeast, there is also liquid yeast, which comes in two forms. The first is in what looks like a large test tube. You can shake it, and dump it into your wort. This is yeast in a culture, so it is already active and ready to go. You should refrigerate this until you are ready to pitch it. This slows down the yeast and keeps them fresh. You should allow liquid yeast to reach room temperature before you pitch it.

The other kind of liquid yeast is packaged in what is sometimes called a punch pack. It looks like a foil juice pack, and inside you can feel a bubble, known as a yeast activator, move around. Inside this activator is the yeast. Pop the bubble by hitting it on a counter with your hand. Yeast is activated when the bubble breaks. Liquid yeast costs about $5; dry yeast only costs about $1. The only advantage is that you get a rapid, strong fermentation with liquid yeast. There is not much difference as far as the quality and the taste of the beer.

Grain

You should now be familiar with the process of growing and producing grains for use in home brewing. *In Chapter 8, you will learn how to use these grains in a process called mashing, or all-grain brewing.* In this process, you will use hot water to extract sugars produced in the kilning process and released into the wort to be used as food for yeast and add sweetness to your beer.

Hops

As mentioned in the Chapter 4, hops were not always used in beer. Other herbs were added for their bitter flavor. Not only do hops add flavor, but they are also a natural preservative. They add flavor and special aromas as well. While they are not essential in the fermentation process, can you really imagine a beer without them? Even though many American-style lagers contain small amounts of bittering hops, they are still there, so they are essential in being able to call most beers "beer." There are, of course, exceptions.

Herbs

Like hops, brewing herbs are not essential in the process of fermentation to a beer, but they offer a huge array of flavor choices. You can experiment, choose your favorites, and even create some new styles of beer on your own. You can try combinations like honey basil ale, horehound brown ale, cholo beer, rhubarb ale, or heather-tip ale.

Home-brew Equipment

Basic home brewing requires some investment. You must be able to mix the main ingredients and store the beer wort while it is fermenting. Once it is done fermenting, you must get the beer into a storage vessel, which is often a glass bottle or keg. Finally, you must cap the bottle to prevent spilling and spoilage.

You may wish to buy other equipment, like kegging or mashing systems, once you produce your first few batches of beer. *The process of mashing will be explained in more detail in Chapter 8.* Once the home-brewing bug bites you, many different upgrades can make home brewing easier and faster, and will allow you to produce larger quantities.

In each of the recipes in this book, you will notice one of the ingredients listed is "standard home-brew equipment." Let us begin with the pieces of equipment that are absolutely necessary in order to make the most basic extract beer. The term extract means that the process of removing the sugars from the grains is already done, and the result is a liquid or dry malt extract. You could get away with a trash can, a hose, and empty soda bottles, but the likelihood of your beer turning out bad increases dramatically.

Here is the list of standard home-brew equipment:

- brew pot
- spoon
- primary fermentation vessel (also doubles as a bottling bucket)
- secondary fermentation vessel (carboy)
- sanitizer
- bottles
- caps
- capper

Each of these will be discussed in the following sections.

"For boiling the wort, I use a stainless steel pot that most people prob-
ably use for lobsters. For fermentation, I usually use a white plastic
brew bucket, although occasionally I use a glass carboy. I almost never
take the specific gravity of the wort or the finished brew, although I
have the gauge. I bottle my beer rather than use a keg."
—Lawrence Shatkin, long-time home brewer, Titusville, N.J.

Brew pot

One of the first things you will do when creating a beer is to boil the malt extract, hops, water, and herbs in a large pot. A brew pot can be any large, stainless steel stockpot that has at least a 9-gallon capacity. You need to have a pot that you only use for home brewing because you do not want any food flavors like pasta sauce leeching into your beer.

You can get away with going to a store like Walmart and buying a pot for $50 or less. You can purchase special brew pots that have a hose attachment and a temperature gauge from a home-brew supply store for $300 or more. It just depends on how fancy and serious you want to be about home brewing. Most home brewers interviewed for this book own just the stainless steel stockpot.

Another pot that has recently become popular over the past few years is the one made for deep-frying a turkey. You can buy the pot and burner for about $50. Do not use one that you have fried a turkey in because you are likely to have oil leech into your beer. Buy one that is dedicated to home brewing.

A turkey fryer is recommended another reason, and that is the burner. It hooks up to a propane gas canister that you would use with most gas grills. This means that you would have to brew outside, but this is good for two main reasons:

1. When the wort starts boiling, it will create a foam that, no matter how careful you are, will boil out of your pot, which also means all over your stove. It creates a sticky mess. When you brew outside on the patio, you can clean up with a hose when you are done.

2. You need to be able to heat a large amount of liquid to the boiling point. Most electric stoves are just not up to the job because they cannot get hot enough. With the burner, you can control the amount of flame, the wort will boil quicker, and you will have more control over keeping it at a high

temperature for the amount of time you will need to do so.

Spoon

You should have equipment solely used for home brewing and no other tasks. You do not want to use the same spoon that you used to stir last night's chili. You can purchase a brew spoon with a long handle made from plastic or stainless steel. You should not use a wooden spoon because bacteria can hide in the pores, no matter how much you clean it. Of the two options, the stainless steel is recommended because the plastic spoon can get scratches that can hide bacteria, and metal can withstand heat much better. You can purchase one from a home-brew supplier. They are usually long enough to stir must in a fermenter and brew pot, and they are easy to clean and sterilize. You will use a spoon for the following activities:

- Stir in yeast when you pitch it into the wort.

- Skim off the foam when you are boiling the wort

- Stir and mix beer ingredients.

- If you need to heat any ingredients on the stove you will need to stir so that it does not burn.

- You should stir a must to aerate it for yeast to begin fermenting.

- Stir and dissolve dry ingredients, such as dried malt extract.

- Remove hops, herbs, cheesecloth, or bag from the fermentation vessel.

Primary fermentation vessel

The beer wort needs somewhere to sit and ferment. There are two types of fermentation systems. The closed fermentation system is recommended because there is less chance of contamination. It is the most common type to use for beer unless you are trying to create a special sour or lambic-style beer that uses wild yeasts as part of the fermentation process.

Open fermentation

Since our ancestors did not understand the concept of microorganisms, they were not sure how fermentation worked. They knew that leaving certain liquids out would change them, but to them it was a magical process. They would place grain and herbs in large, open vessels, and the wild yeast would begin fermentation on its own. Many of these early batches were likely mostly grainy vinegar, but over time, man discovered the existence of microorganisms, such as bacteria and yeasts.

To our ancestors, this process was so mystical they felt that the secrets of fermentation belonged to the gods and goddesses of their culture. There would be great festivals held in the honor of gods like Bacchus, the Greek god of wine and intoxication, which were celebrated for days, and sometimes even weeks. Storage techniques were still rudimentary, so the beer was quickly consumed.

An open fermentation system means that the vessel where the wort is fermenting is not sealed. You can use a large plastic or glass container and create lambics this way.

I have tried open fermentation with some marginal success. I had a large plastic bucket and covered it with a trash bag. The bag was not used to seal it, but it did keep bugs out. It was a rather weak, tart beer. One of my first fermentation vessels was a bucket that looked like a large pickle barrel with a metal wire handle. This is what most primary fermentation vessels look like.

The main criterion of a plastic home-brew vessel is that it must be made of food-grade plastic. *You can purchase this at a hardware store, a home-brew supply store, or you can also order online through the sources mentioned in Appendix B.* Do not use a bucket that has been used for any other purpose. If there were any chemicals stored in the bucket, they can leach into your beer.

You may want to buy a bucket with a hole drilled near the bottom. It should cost less than $5. The existence of the hole allows you to screw on a plastic spigot so that you can easily move the beer from one vessel to another. Most of the fermentation buckets you purchase at home-brew supply stores already have the hole. You will need a spigot to attach to the bucket. If you buy a bucket from a hardware store, you will have to drill the hole yourself, and measure it so the spigot will fit.

Bacteria, fruit flies, and other nasty bugs love open fermentation, which is why it is not recommended. Oxidation is another problem with open vessel fermentation. When your beer becomes oxidized, it will lose its color, turn brown, and spoil.

Tip: *Some fermenters have marks on them to indicate 1-, 5-, and 6-gallon levels. If yours does not, fill the bucket with water at the different levels, and mark these delineations both on the inside and outside of the bucket with a permanent marker.*

Glass carboy containers used in beer fermentation are not recommended for open fermentation systems, as the top opening is not wide enough to allow healthy yeast to find its way to your beer.

Closed fermentation

In order to create a closed fermentation, you will need to add a lid to your fermentation vessel. Most plastic fermentation vessels have lids that pop on top and have a rubber gasket to create an airtight seal. When you purchase a fermentation bucket from a supply store, the lid is usually included.

You should look on top of the lid to make sure you find another small hole. This is where the gas will escape. If you ever cooked with a pressure cooker, you saw the small release valve on the top. Carbon dioxide gas is released during fermentation, and without the hole, you will create a gas bomb. Eventually, the pressure will pop the lid off and make a mess.

If the lid does not have a hole, many supply stores will drill the hole for you. A rubber ring in this hole creates a seal for the inserted fermentation lock. The fermentation lock is another small item that will need to be purchased. It is relatively cheap, but it serves a very important purpose. It allows gas to escape, but, at the same time, keeps oxygen and other unwanted visitors from finding their way into your fermentation vessel. One end has a small pipe that fits into the top hole in the fermenter lid. On top is a place to put sterilized water.

When your beer is fermenting, you will see bubbles created from the carbon dioxide in your fermentation lock. It will provide you with important information. First, it will tell you when fermentation begins, and, second, when it ends. You should change the water in your fermentation lock every couple of days. Make sure it is sanitized or distilled water.

   Tip: *Reduce the number of times you open the lid of your fermenter. Each time you open it, there is a risk of contamination.*

Do not forget to place your fermentation lock on your fermenter. Imagine shaking a bottle of cola; when you open the lid, the liquid comes showering out. This same thing will happen if you forget to put on the fermentation lock.

Carboy

Another kind of fermenter often used is called a carboy. This is a large glass bottle with a small neck. It works the same as a plastic bucket, except that instead of a lid with a hole in it, you place a rubber stopper, or bung. Bungs are drilled with a hole so that a fermentation lock can be placed into the top.

Secondary fermentation occurs after the primary fermentation ceases. Once the rapid bubbling and frothing has stopped, the beer is usually transferred to the carboy and racked off its trub.

If you are making beer on a budget, you can get away with just one vessel and doing only primary fermentation, or you can use two buckets instead of a carboy. Beer taste can improve over time in the bottle, but it takes longer, and you risk having a lot of sediment in your bottles. Leftover trub can add unpleasant flavor, and things floating in the beer might turn some people off.

There is some advantage to using a carboy, and it has to do with the shape of the container. Oxygen is bad because it oxidizes the beer, and it can change the color and flavor of your finished product. Bad bacteria love oxygen and can spoil your beer in an oxygen-rich environment. Since a carboy is cone-shaped at the top, it reduces the **headspace** in the beer. The headspace is the area between the top of your beer and the top of the vessel. One of the gasses released from beer is nitrogen, which preserves beer and prevents spoilage. When you seal your carboy, the nitrogen will naturally form a barrier and, therefore, buffer your beer. It has less of an area to occupy in a carboy. The tighter you seal your carboy, the better your beer will be, because you contain the nitrogen and disallow oxygen from coming into contact with your beer.

Another way to reduce headspace is to add beer that has already been brewed and bottled to your carboy. Be sure it is the same type of beer. Evaporation occurs naturally, and you will lose a little bit of your beer when you rack it off the trub. The less headspace you leave, the better the chance you will have a perfect beer.

There are carboys of all sizes to choose from, and there are also demijohns, which are one step bigger. Two recipes in this book use a 5- to 6-gallon carboy. The standard equipment includes the 5-gallon carboy. When shopping for a bung to go into your carboy, you must make sure it is the right size, and that it has a hole drilled into it. Most home brewing supply stores can help you with this. You will use the same fermentation lock that you would use with the bucket type of fermenter.

> **Tip:** *Be careful lifting your carboy. They are glass and do not have a handle. A full carboy of beer can weigh close to 50 pounds. You should get someone to help you lift your fermenter. There will be times you will need to lift it off the ground to a greater height. When you are racking off beer into another fermenter, a siphon will only work if the carboy you are racking from is higher than the fermenter that the clear beer is being siphoned into. You can buy a carboy handle that attaches to your carboy, which will make lifting easier.*

Your fermenters are your most essential implements. A couple of other standard items are recommended in order to make the best beer possible. You could get away with not having these items, but you increase the risk of a bad batch of beer.

Sanitizer

Repeat this mantra over and over again: "Clean your parts before you start."

You must always clean and sanitize every piece of equipment, including your hands, before coming in contact with your beer. You must sanitize every time you move your beer from one vessel to another, and your bottles must be sanitized before you fill them.

Two types of sanitizers recommended for cleaning your equipment are B-Brite™ and C-Brite™, which come in powdered form. You dissolve a small amount of the powder in water and use the water to clean everything you are working with, including your hands. You can never sanitize something too much. The sanitizing solution will kill any bacteria or microorganisms that could hurt your beer. The great thing about these products is that you do not have to rinse the equipment after you sanitize. The sanitizer will not hurt you or the beer. These products have an iodine base, which gives it killing power; if you are sensitive to iodine, you might want to consider some other product.

You should try not to use chlorine products, as this will leave an aftertaste in your beer. If you do choose to use chlorine, you should use it in diluted amounts, like 1 teaspoon per 1 gallon of water. Never use soap to clean your equipment. Your beer will taste soapy because soap will leave a residue on your equipment. Use the hottest water you can stand. You can even fill your dishwasher with your equipment, and instead of washing powder, you can use sanitizer. This also works well for sterilizing bottles before filling them.

If you have a question about whether or not to sanitize it; then sanitize it. Remember your cleaning mantra; post it where you can see it when you make your beer. You should only use your beer-making equipment for making beer. Do not use it for anything else. You should always clean and sanitize your equipment before you store it, and try to store it dry. When you use stored equipment, you will need to sanitize it again.

Bottles

You could leave the beer in a fermenter and drink it directly from there, but you would need to drink it quickly, because as the headspace grows, your beer will spoil and go flat. It would be tough to pour it from a carboy, but you could rack it back into the primary fermentation bucket and dispense it from the bottom.

I would recommend that you only store beer in bottles or a keg. Bottles last longer, they are easy to store, and you can keep them cool, which reduces spoilage. Keeping bottles in a cool place also reduces the chance of re-fermentation and popping bottles.

In beer making, bottles can be the most expensive thing you will ever have to buy. You can buy them from home-brew supply stores. They are expensive to purchase online because of the shipping costs. *I tell my friends that I will replace their empties with full bottles.*

When choosing bottles, you should use a type that do not have a screw top and that are colored, not clear.

You will not be able to put a cap on a screw top bottle, so you do not need to save any of these types of bottles. They do not work in a capper. *I recommend you be kind to the environment and recycle them.* You need standard-sized 12-ounce or 22-ounce bottles, as these are the easiest to work with.

Clear bottles can spoil beer and cause off-flavors and coloring when they are struck by light. This is called "light-struck beer" and has a skunk-like odor due to a chemical reaction that occurs when beer is exposed to too much light. Beer bottles come in all different colors; so, you can choose your favorite to keep or give as special gifts once you have filled them.

Do not use wine bottles to bottle beer. You might be able to get a cap on them, but they cannot withstand the pressure caused by the carbonation build up that occurs after beer is bottled.

Ask your friends and family to save beer bottles for you. You might want to think of a place to store them because soon you can be overrun with them. You will need 54 12-ounce bottles to make one 5-gallon batch of beer.

If you are still having difficulty locating bottles after you have asked friends and family; then you can ask the owners at local a bar, pub, or restaurant for their empty bottles of beer. Most of them just recycle their bottles at the end of the night; so ask them to hold them, and you will pick them up. You can also ask the bar owners for the boxes the beer came in. They are a great item to store empty bottles and beer in. You can pick through and re-cycle the bottles you do not need or cannot use. You are doing the world a favor by recycling. You probably never thought you could be environmentally responsible by sipping a home brew.

There are two different types of home brewers: Those who care about labels stuck on used beer bottles, and those who do not. *To be honest, I started out the first type and, over time, became the second type. Here are some of the tricks I learned:*

1. Steaming the labels or pouring hot water over them will loosen most labels, but not all. The glue used on labels today is tough. Labels on beer bottles are much easier to remove than those on wine bottles. The reason they make them so hard to remove is that wine is supposed to last for decades, so the label must last that long as well. The hotter the water, the easier it will be to get the label off.

2. You can use a hair dryer to heat the label and try to peel it off that way. This does not work as well as using water and heat.

3. Have you ever noticed that when a bottle of beer is placed in an ice cooler, the label will slip right off? You can try to put your bottles in a cooler with ice and water.

4. You can try some abrasive cleaner or steel wool. Make sure you rinse the bottle really well after using these methods. This method can usually get off a tough label when combined with heat and water.

5. Try soaking it in water with a little ammonia or dish soap added.

6. You can soak bottles in wallpaper remover. Make sure that you rinse the bottles well before using them.

7. If you really want a clean bottle, you may need to use a razor to scratch it off. Be very careful.

Tip: *Some Web sites suggest using gasoline as a solvent. Never do this. Gasoline is dangerous and has no business in home beer making.*

You can create your own labels on the computer, print them out, and paste them over the old label.

Tip: *Scraping off beer labels is a lot of work, and I gave up. I would rather drink the beer than make sure the bottle looks perfect. I did make a mistake in my relinquishment, and that was that I did not bother to label the bottles in any discernable way. This became a problem because when I made more than one batch of beer, I forgot* *which bottle contained a particular beer. I began marking the top of caps. This was fine as long as I remembered what my scrawl meant six months later. There was a time I brewed two beers at the same time. One beer was a Canadian beer and one was a Mexican beer. I decided that the Canadian beer tasted like Molson and the Mexican tasted like Corona beer. So, I put either a "C" or an "M" on the tops of the beer caps. At the time, it seemed like pure genius, but a couple of months later I looked at the caps and thought, "What does the C and M stand for? Do they represent Mexican and Canadian or do they mean Molson and Corona?" Not one of my brighter moments. In the end, I just put them all in an ice bucket and invited friends over. The beer disappeared, and no one really cared. I learned my lesson about labeling bottles.*

It is best to put some type of label on your bottles. It does not have to be fancy; it just has to say what it is in it.

Caps

These are flat caps lined with a rubber seal. You can buy bags of hundreds for about $5 at many home-brew supply shops. You can buy plain caps or fancy ones with art on them.

Capper

You will use this tool to crimp your cap onto the beer bottle. It has two handles and a magnet in the center of the crimping ring. The magnet holds the cap on the bottle while you push the handles down to crimp the cap into place. A hand capper costs about $20 at most home-brew supply stores.

Intermediate Supplies

There is some equipment that would be on the list of immediate upgrades. These are not serious upgrades like the list in the advanced section; rather, they are small items that can allow you to control the results of your beer making and make some of the actions much easier. These are not usually included in beginner home-brew kits, unless you are lucky.

Here is a list of intermediate supplies:

- bottle brushes
- bottle filler
- hydrometer
- floating thermometer
- tubing
- additives

Each of these is detailed in the following sections.

Bottle brushes

In order to clean bottles and carboys, you can buy bottle brushes. The sediment that forms on the bottom of bottles and carboys can be hard to shake loose with just simple rinsing. Bottle brushes come in different sizes. You can buy a smaller one for your bottles and a long, large one for your carboy. You can bend the handle slightly on the long brush before inserting into your carboy so that you can get to all the edges and corners. The bend is especially helpful in cleaning the upper part of the carboy.

You should use your bottle brush on your bottles, especially if they are used bottles, before you sanitize them. Use really hot water and fill the beer bottle. Use the brush to clean the bottle of any sediment. Hold the bottle up to a bright light so that you are sure you got everything. If you leave sediment, you are asking for trouble later on.

After using your carboy in fermentation, fill the carboy about a quarter full with hot water, and use the brush to clean the bottom and the sides. Without a brush, this is almost impossible unless you fill the carboy with really hot water and let it soak a long time. Even then, you will have difficulty.

Do not use your brush on a plastic primary fermenter. Brushes can cause scratches in the plastic, creating a place for microorganisms to hide. You should never use any kind of abrasive on a plastic fermenter.

Bottle filler

A bottle filler, in some ways, belongs on the essentials list. You can get by without having one, but once you have one, you will wonder why you did not buy it earlier. When filling bottles from a fermenter, you have to cut off the flow manually. Most people will likely dribble some on the floor in the process, which makes a sticky mess.

The bottle filler fits on the end of your tubing. It is a long plastic pipe that fits into the beer bottle. At the end of the pipe is a spring mechanism. When you push the pipe down, it allows the beer to flow. When you release the pressure, the flow stops. Placing something like an old towel on the floor underneath your beer bottles is recommended, as you will have some spillage.

Tip: *From past experience, I would recommend that you have special home-brew clothes. Beer can stain and malt is sticky. One time I was wearing a relatively new pair of leather shoes. I was making mead — a type of honey wine — and somehow honey dripped on the top of these shoes. The shoes were ruined, and my wife was not happy. Every time she saw me getting ready to make wine or beer, she told me to put on my honey shoes. Those shoes became the official home-brew loafers.*

The other function of the bottle filler is to create headspace. While excess headspace in your carboy is bad; in the case of bottles, a little headspace is necessary. Look at any commercial beer. You will see a space between the top of the liquid and the cork. This is to allow some off-gassing of the beer. Beer will release some gasses while it is in the bottle. If you do not allow some room, the gases will make room by exploding the bottle; it is a matter of physics. The bottle filler takes up some room in the bottle when it is inserted. Even if you fill the bottle to the top with beer, when you remove the filler, there will be some space left in the bottle. It is the perfect amount of headspace. *Trust me; it would not be fun to recreate Old Faithful. Beer is always better in your mouth than all over the floor.*

Bottle fillers usually cost less than $20. It might be a good idea to buy one early in order to save you time, mess, and aggravation.

Hydrometer

At the beginning of all of the recipes, you will see the letters OG and FG. OG stands for "original gravity" and FG represents "final gravity." These letters are followed by a number and are important because they lead to the ABV, or "alcohol by volume." Remember that yeast eats sugar and converts it into alcohol. The amount of fermentable sugar in a beer will determine how much alcohol a certain beer should contain when it has finished fermenting. Another abbreviation you might see is SG, or "specific gravity." This is a reading you will take during the process of fermentation to determine if the beer has finished fermenting or if it might be a stuck fermentation.

OG represents the first reading you take at the time you pitch the yeast in the beer. This helps determine the potential of alcohol a beer will have. FG represents the last hydrometer reading before you bottle your beer. This is important because you can use it to determine what the actual amount of sugar has been converted to alcohol by subtracting the FG from the OG. The resulting number is the potential alcohol in your beer. More sophisticated instruments are used in breweries, but for home brewers, this system is more than sufficient.

This is important to know for a couple of reasons. First, when you are fixing your beer at the beginning and preparing it for fermentation, knowing the original gravity will help you determine if you need any more malt or if the mixture needs a little dilution. Knowing the final gravity will help you determine when fermentation is over. If your beer has not quite reached the final gravity, it could mean that your fermentation is stuck, you picked the wrong kind of yeast, or that it is still quietly fermenting. If you bottle your beer too soon, it could be too sweet, not have enough alcohol for taste, or continue to ferment in the bottle.

In order to understand specific gravity, think in terms of density. Try this experiment to help you understand how it works:

1. Fill a beer bottle to the top with water.

2. Place an unsharpened pencil, eraser side down, into the water. It will float.

3. Mark on the pencil where the top of the bottle is.

4. Empty the water into a container and add a cup of sugar to it. Mix it well so that the sugar dissolves.

5. Fill the bottle with the sugar water.

6. Place the pencil eraser side down into the liquid. You will notice that the line you marked on the pencil the first time is higher above the water line. This is because the mixture of water and sugar is denser than plain water.

The pencil you used in the experiment is a crude, but effective, hydrometer. Hydrometers are sealed glass tubes with a paper label inside them. In the bottom is usually mercury or some other heavy metal to weigh it down, just like the eraser. There are usually three different scales, but the one that shows specific gravity is the one that has 1.000 and numbers above and below 1.000. This number, 1.000, is the specific gravity of plain water. Readings higher than 1.000 indicate liquids are denser than water. Readings on the scale of .999 or lower indicate liquids are less dense than water. What is less dense than water? Alcohol. You could repeat the pencil experiment and pour rubbing alcohol into the bottle. The pencil will sink lower than the line for plain water.

On many hydrometers, there are two other scales. These scales are Balling scale or Brix, and potential alcohol of your beer. The Brix scale shows you how much sugar there is in a liquid. In order to use the potential alcohol content, you can do a reading of the potential alcohol before it ferments; then after it is finished. You then subtract the two numbers. All three of these scales use the same process for determining what the specific gravity of a liquid is, but each scale is just another way of reading it. It is similar to a thermometer that has both Fahrenheit and Celsius scales. These are both measurements of the same level of mercury.

If it is 10 percent before and 4 percent after, the potential alcohol content of your beer is about 6 percent. This works because the sugar was converted to alcohol, and the amount of change of the gravity is alcohol replacing the sugar. This potential alcohol is the same as the ABV number on the recipe. The Balling reading refers to sugar content in your mixture. It is assumed that your must is denser because of the amount of sugar in it. When you are finished with your beer, your balling will be lower.

You need to concentrate on the specific gravity. If you want to determine what the alcohol content will be before you make a beer and only have OG and FG, you can use this standard formula. You need to plug in the final and original gravities.

Approximate Alcohol Content (%) = $\dfrac{\text{FG} - \text{OG}}{0.0074}$

The ABV has already been calculated for you in each recipe. It is important to know the potential alcohol content of a beer because it will help you decide which yeast to use.

If your beer has a potential alcohol content of 8 percent, but you are using yeast that dies out at 4 percent, then you will produce a sweet beer with less alcohol. You may desire less alcohol in your beer, but alcohol does significantly contribute to the overall taste of a beer. Having too much or too little alcohol can make a beer weak or overpowering.

Be aware that temperature can alter a hydrometer reading. You should always try to read a hydrometer at room temperature. If it is too cool or hot, your reading can be off because liquid contracts when it gets hot and becomes denser when it cools. Here is an adjustment scale.

°F Adjust
40 - .002
50 - .001
60 0
70 + .001
80 + .002
90 + .004
100 + .005
110 + .007
120 + .008
130 + .010
140 + .013
150 + .015

You should also purchase a hydrometer-testing jar. This makes it easier to read and uses only a small amount of beer. You should always clean your equipment after use, but never return a beer sample back into the fermenter. You can taste it if you like and dump the rest when you are done. *I have found that tasting the beer during the different stages of fermentation has helped me learn what it should taste and smell like. This helps me determine when a beer is done or when there is a problem that needs to be fixed.*

Tip: *When testing to see if a beer has stopped fermenting, you should not just rely on one reading. Test it over a couple of days, and if the reading remains constant, then it has stopped. If it is still changing, you should wait until it has completely stopped fermenting before you consider bottling the beer.*

Floating thermometer

The temperature of your beer is very important for fermentation and brewing. If your beer is too hot or too cold, the yeast will die off or go into a suspended state. If you kill the yeast, you will have to start all over again. When brewing a beer, you want to attain a certain temperature and hold it for a certain amount of time. This is important in transforming the bittering agents in the hops.

If you could dedicate a temperature-controlled room for fermenting your beer, this would be optimal. Most people must use their kitchen, bathroom, garage, or outbuilding for their hobby. These areas are a little harder to control the temperature in.

Before pitching the yeast into a beer must, you must make sure it is as close to room temperature as possible, or maybe a little above. Do not pitch the yeast above 75 degrees Fahrenheit. If you can keep the must at about 68 degrees Fahrenheit during primary fermentation, this is a good temperature for healthy yeast growth. If you drop below 60 degrees Fahrenheit, your yeast will go dormant.

Floating thermometers work the best for testing beer. You can place them in the fermenter to take a direct reading. The other time you might want to check the temperature is before taking a hydrometer reading so that you get as accurate a reading as possible.

The fact that the thermometer floats makes it easy to read and retrieve. You might want to tie a monofilament string on the top loop so that your hand does not go anywhere near the must. Remember to sanitize the thermometer every time you use it.

If your must is not the right temperature, here are some suggestions.

- Buy a Brew Belt or a FermWrap heater. These wrap around the fermenter and allow you adjust the heat of the must. The FermWrap will work on a plastic bucket or a carboy. A Brew Belt is not recommended for use on a glass carboy. They are less than $30 and plug into the wall.

- Wrap the fermenter in a blanket. Do not use an electric blanket because it is not safe.

- Wrap insulation around your fermenter. It will keep the must at a constant temperature; however, insulation is easily ruined if it gets wet.

- Wrap the fermenter in foam rubber. This works similar to insulation, but it can get wet and be washed.

- If it is too hot, place the fermenter in an ice bath. This will cool it quickly and is not recommended for use during rapid fermentation.

- Place in a basement or spring house. A spring house is a small building outside that contains a natural spring and usually has a pump inserted. These small buildings are sometimes partially underground; they are usually cool and have a constant temperature because the water is cold. The constant temperature is especially necessary if you are creating a lager.

- Place a wet T-shirt over your fermenter and place a fan next to it. This homemade air conditioning system will cool it quickly, but is not recommended during fermentation.

- A wort chiller is copper tubing that is inserted into the liquid with cold water running through it. The heat from the liquid is transferred out of the liquid with the flowing water. This is a quick way to drop the temperature in order to get it close to the temperature needed to pitch the yeast.

Tubing

There are a number of beginning home-brew kits that include tubing. You will find that it is almost essential in transferring beer to another vessel, and it is needed for transferring beer into bottles. You can buy this item from the hardware store. You need to measure the diameter of your spigot and bottle filler before you purchase it. Also, make sure that it is food-grade flexible tubing. It is relatively cheap, so buy it by the yard. It is an item that is very difficult to clean, so if there is any buildup, you should recycle it and cut a new piece of tubing.

Before cutting the tubing, measure out how much you will need to go from the fermenter to a bottle or another fermenter. Once you cut it, you cannot tape it back together, so take the time to measure it first. You can have a couple of different sets of tubing in order to use them for different tasks.

Before I use the tubing, I fill a container with sanitizer and soak the tubing. Then I run hot water through the tubing as well. When I am finished using the tubing, I repeat this process, make sure that there is not water in the tube; then hang it up to dry.

Additives

Chemicals you can add to your beer to make it clear are called clarifiers. An example is Irish moss. If you have hard water, you might consider adding a water conditioner, such as gypsum or Burton salts. These additives condition the water without hurting the flavor of your beer.

In order to help your yeast out, you can add yeast nutrient and yeast energizer. Each of these can help a stuck or slow fermentation. Each of these additives cost only a few dollars. Before adding any of these, you should question whether you really need them, as some of them have the potential to produce odd flavors.

Advanced Supplies

Are you ready to upgrade? Are you a "gear" junkie? *In this section, you will find a list of equipment that is either an upgrade of your current equipment or is additional equipment that can help you in your quest to make better beer.*

Here is a list of upgrades and beer gear:

- floor capper
- pail opening tool
- bottle washer
- bottle tree
- kegs
- transfer pump
- siphon
- upgrade faucets
- alcohol tester
- fancy labels

Each of these is explained in detail in the following sections.

Floor/ bench capper

Are your hands and back tired yet from crimping caps onto bottles? There is an easier way. A bench and a floor capper work the same way. One can sit on your counter, and the other is tall and can be used on the floor. Many of these come from Italy and have a durable design, so you will never have to replace them. They are capable of capping up to about 150 bottles per hour. You pull down the arm and the bottle is perfectly capped without any damage. Sometimes you can end up butchering caps using a hand unit. These units sell for around $100.

Pail opening tool

This can make getting the lid off a plastic fermenter much easier. It is a metal hand tool that can get up and under the lid and save your fingers from getting hurt trying to pry off the lid. This life-saving device goes for about $5. *I have one and could not live without it.*

Bottle washer

This piece of equipment can screw onto the faucet where you clean your bottles and carboy. It puts the water under pressure to clean better, and it has a push trigger that only releases water when you press your bottle or carboy onto it.

Bottle tree

This is a quick way to sanitize and store bottles. It is a tower. You place your bottle on branches that stick out. This keeps the bottles upside down to dry and keeps them cleaner. Some models have an attachment that will spray sanitizer up into the bottles before you hang them.

Kegs

Have you ever imagined being able to create draft beer at home? You can when you buy a kegging system. The initial cost can be close to $1,000, but once you have the equipment, you just have to replace the CO_2 tank from time to time. Beer from a keg is fresh, never flat, and is really impressive to your friends.

There are benefits and considerations you should take into account before investing in a kegging system. There is, of course, the benefit of convenience and control over your beer. The convenience is that you do not have hundreds of bottles lying around your house, and you do not have to wait for your bottles to condition. Conditioning is the process of adding a little priming sugar to the beer before you bottle it. The residual yeast will create carbon dioxide in the form of bubbles and a head on your beer. You will have the control of adding the carbonation directly to the beer at the rate you choose. This creates consistent beer, glass after glass. You may not find the same consistency in bottle-conditioned beer.

The drawback, of course, is the price, and you will need room to set up your kegging system. You will need enough room to store and refrigerate your kegs. The good news is that kegs come in all different sizes, even small 5-liter mini-keg sizes. These can fit easily into your refrigerator. If you have larger kegs, you may need a special beer refrigerator just to store and cool your kegs.

You will need a number of components to set up a home keg system:

Keg

You can buy a 5-gallon soda canister, originally manufactured by the Cornelius Company of Osseo, Minnesota. These are often referred to as Corny kegs. There are other brands such as Firestone brand made by Spartanburg Steel Products, Spartanburg, South Carolina, however the hardware that is needed may not fit both a corny keg and a different brand. You can buy used kegs from soda or beer companies. You can also purchase kegs or whole keg systems from larger home brew supply stores.

The kegs most home brewers use are 8 ½ inches in diameter, about 26 inches tall, and hold 5 gallons of beer. On the top and bottom are plastic caps that can absorb shock as they are moved from one place to another. Usually, the top cap has handles that make the kegs easy to lift. You want to make sure that you buy a keg that has a pressure-relief valve in the lid, as this is an extremely important safety feature. An exploding keg would be very dangerous and create quite a mess.

You can buy two types of kegs: a ball-lock and a pin-lock. These terms refer to the how the fittings connect to the valves and hoses. You must be sure that you have the right kind of fittings for the type of keg you have purchased. These two systems are not interchangeable. Of the two systems, the ball-locks are easy to take apart with a socket set. When buying a system, consider buying two kegs because you do not want to have to wait to keg a beer while you are drinking from another one.

CO_2 container

This is a pressurized gas canister that adds the bubble to your beer. You can purchase this from a local beer or soda supply company or even a gas company. When you purchase a tank, make sure that there is a stamp with a certification date on top that indicates a pressure test has been performed. This test is usually good for five years before it has to be tested again. This does not mean you have to have it tested every time it is filled; it is merely a test to show that the tank is in good working condition. This ensures that the tank is safe to use. If you do not see a certification or the person that you are buying the tank from cannot provide one, then do not buy the tank.

Regulator

This lowers the pressure of the gas from the CO_2 tank as it travels to the keg. Both single and dual-gauge styles work perfectly well. Both include a gauge that indicates the output (low) pressure setting, which is the most important information you need.

Regulators come in a single- or dual-gauge type. These gauges will regulate or drop the pressure of the gas from 800 pounds per square inch from the tank to the 10 to 30 pounds per square inch you will need for carbonation and dispensing. You can adjust the regulator to control how much carbonation there is and how fast it will be dispensed.

The dual-gauge type has a gauge that is dedicated to the pressure of the tank. This will let you know how much gas is left in the tank and when it is time to consider replacing a tank for a full one. Once you buy a tank, you can exchange full ones for empty ones when you purchase more gas.

Hoses

You will need one to connect the keg to the CO_2 and one to a faucet or tap to dispense the beer. You can purchase hoses the same place you purchase tanks and fittings. These are specialized hoses that operate under pressure.

Fittings

As mentioned previously, kegs come in two types: ball-lock and pin-lock. You will need to purchase disconnect fittings for whatever type of keg you have. You can, however, purchase a flare-style outlet. This will allow you to connect to pin-lock or ball-lock fittings to your regulator and allows you to connect to more than one keg at a time.

Transfer pumps

These pump beer from one vessel to another quickly. They are electrical units that can pump one to three gallons a minute and come with a price tag of about $200.

Siphon

Siphons are a much cheaper alternative to a pump. A beer siphon is a long tube within a tube that, when depressed, starts beer moving from one vessel to another. These cost less than $20. The alternative is sucking the beer through the tube to start the beer flowing. Not the most sanitary way to move beer — although it is the tastiest.

Upgrade faucets

You can change the faucet on your fermenters to a high-flow lever faucet. You may even consider an inline faucet. This can be placed between two pieces of tubing and give you control over the flow. Each of these only cost a few dollars.

Fancy labels

People get very creative with labels. You can buy pre-gummed labels that you just wet and stick on. You can also buy plain sheets of label paper to be used in your printer. You can create whatever style or design you like. There are even label contests at beer competitions. Some of the pre-made labels and label papers can be a little pricey.

I use regular printer paper and school paste to put on my labels. This is for two reasons: one is that after making thousands of bottles, I got a little tired of making fancy labels. The other reason is that paste from a bottle is much easier to use than a pre-gummed label. I do recommend you use some sort of label.

Labels can really dress up your bottle, and you can give them as gifts. An advantage to using label paper is that it does not disintegrate when it is exposed to liquid like paper labels will.

Home-brew kits

If you are ready to create a beer, you should buy a home-brew kit either online or at a home-brew supply store locally. They usually contain the essential equipment for creating a beer. These are usually more cost-effective than buying each part individually. Many of the kits will offer upgrades like caps, a capper, or a carboy.

Once you have all your equipment, it is time to try out your first batch. The good news is that buying a beer recipe kit will take all the guesswork out of brewing beer. The first recipe kit you should purchase is an extract kit. This means that all the grains have been processed. These kits use a malt extract (in dry or syrup form), hops, liquid or dry yeast, and instructions. Many contain priming sugar, and if they do not, you might have to buy some from the home-brew supplier. You will need caps and bottles, or if you are adventurous, a keg system. These kits will yield 5 gallons of beer. Many of these kits will come in hundreds of different styles of beer. The instructions in these kits are usually thorough, and most of these kits have been tried hundreds of times, so unless you make a big mistake, you will be able to create a ready-to-drink batch of beer in about three weeks.

The next level of beer kit is an extract kit with specialty grains. This is close to the type of beer you can create using the grains from your garden. The grains they contain are for the purpose of flavor rather than adding fermentable sugars. These grains are placed in a sock-like bag and boiled for a specified time. They also add color and are necessary for darker beers.

You do not necessarily need a kit to create an extract beer. You can use a beer recipe and purchase the components yourself, or when you become really advanced, you can create new recipes on your own.

In the beginning of Chapter 8, you will learn step-by-step instructions for creating an extract with specialty grains and all-grain beer along with some recipes of each type.

Chapter 8

Home Brewing Extract with Specialty Grains

"This is grain, which any fool can eat, but for which the Lord intended a more divine means of consumption... Beer!"
— **Friar Tuck in Robin Hood, Prince of Thieves**

I f you have tried using a kit, you will be familiar with this process of creating a beer. *I am going to use a pale ale as an example of how to create your own extract beer from a recipe.*

Ingredients

- 7 lbs. light malt extract

- 1 lb. 60 L crystal malt

- Grain bag (looks like a sock and can be purchased from a home brew supply store)

- 2 oz. Centennial hops

- 3 oz. Cascade hops

- 1 oz. Irish moss

- 10-lb. bag of ice

- 5 to 6 gal. of water

- American Ale yeast (dry)

- 1 c. of priming sugar

- Standard home-brew equipment *(see list in Chapter 8)*

Instructions

1. Make sure all of your equipment is clean and sanitized.

2. Boil 2 to 2 ½ gallons of water in your brew pot.

3. Make sure the water is about 150 to 155 degrees Fahrenheit.

4. Place your Crystal malt into the small grain bag. Tie a knot in the top so the grain will not come out.

5. When the water is 150 to 155 degrees Fahrenheit, place the bag in the water. Make sure it is completely saturated. Place the lid on the pot. Allow the grains to steep for 30 minutes at this temperature.

6. Remove the grain bag from pot with your spoon. You can then discard it or put it into you compost pile later.

7. Open your bag or can of malt extract, and with your spoon, add it to the pot. Stir this well, and make sure it is all dissolved. You can spoon some hot water into the can or bag, swish it around, and pour into the pot to make sure you get all of the extract. The extract should be very thick, like syrup. Put the pot on the stove or gas burner, and bring to a boil.

8. When the wort begins to boil, set a timer for one hour. You need to sit and watch the brew, as it may boil over. If this happens, you can add some ice cubes and/or turn the heat down for a minute, and then turn it back up. You need to stir as well.

9. Once you set the timer, add your Centennial hops. These can be from your garden, or you can buy them in pellet form. No matter what form, you can put them in a small grain bag or hop bag. These are the same thing except the hop bag is the size of a playing card.

10. While your wort is boiling, make sure that your fermentation vessel is clean and sanitized; you may also want to place your yeast in a glass of lukewarm water.

11. Roughly 45 minutes into your boil, add the Irish moss, and stir in with your spoon. You can also add your Cascade hops. You should place these hops in a hop bag as well.

12. After the hour is complete, carefully remove the hops bags, and cool the wort. You can use an immersion cooler if you have one. If not, fill your sink or bathtub with ice. Place the pot in the ice. You want to cool the wort quickly, because the longer it stands, the more likely it can become contaminated with microbes that will ruin your beer. You may need to add more ice as it melts.

13. You will want to bring the temperature to 80 degrees Fahrenheit. When it has reached this temperature, pour the wort into the primary fermentation vessel.

14. Add cold water until it reaches the 5-gallon level on your bucket.

15. Use your spoon and mix the wort well to get an even temperature.

16. Extract some wort for a sample and use the hydrometer to check the OG. Make a note.

17. Pitch the yeast. This is done by pouring it into the wort and gently stirring it until well mixed.

18. Close the fermenter with your lid. Make sure it has been sanitized. Attach your fermentation lock, which should also be sanitized and filled with sanitized water. Place the fermenter in a dark, dry area that stays at least 70 degrees Fahrenheit.

19. Within the next 24 hours, you will begin to see the fermentation lock bubble. This is a sign that fermentation has begun. It is crucial that the place is warm enough for the yeast to thrive; otherwise, you have a stuck fermentation. If this happens, warm the fermenter with a Fermabelt or warm blanket for a while until you see signs of life.

20. After the initial lively fermentation, which should last a few days, the bubbling will slow down. Check to see fermentation is continuing by using a hydrometer. When the gravity stays the same for a couple of readings in a row, then the fermentation has stopped.

21. You should leave your beer in the primary fermenter for

about two weeks. When you are sure that fermentation has ceased, siphon the beer into your carboy or another bucket.

22. Allow it to sit another 24 hours, and then siphon into a bottling bucket. This is the same as a fermentation bucket. Be sure that it has a spigot on the bottom for bottling.

23. Remember that all the equipment must be sanitized before bottling.

24. Heat 16 ounces of water in a pot, but not to boiling. Stir in priming sugar until dissolved and then set aside with a lid.

25. You may choose to clean and sanitize your bottles in a dishwasher. Instead of dishwasher detergent, use sanitizer. This will only work if the bottles are cleaned out and have no residue or trub inside. If they do, you will need to use a bottle brush and sanitizer. Fill the bottle with hot sanitizer water. Use the brush to clean the bottle. Place the bottle in a bucket of sanitizer until you are ready to fill it with beer.

26. Place your tubing on the spigot and the bottle filler on the bottom of the tubing.

27. Add the priming sugar to the beer and stir

28. Take each bottle and push the filler down until it is full of beer and set aside.

29. Take a cap and stick it to the magnet in the capper with the crimp side down. Place over full bottle and push the arms down. Do this for each of the bottles.

30. When you are done, allow the beer to sit in an area that is about 70 degrees Fahrenheit for 24 hours; then place the beer into a cooler place for another week or two. Then drink and enjoy.

The method described above can be used and adapted for most any type of ale made from extract or extract and specialty grains.

Here are some recipes for creating some of your own ales using grains, hops, and herbs you have grown on your own. If there are herbs in the recipe, you will add them in a grain bag during the last 15 minutes of boiling.

Wit Beer

Ingredients:

- 4 ½ lbs. light dry wheat malt extract

- 2 lbs. orange honey

- 1 oz. Hallertauer or Northern Brewer (7.5 HBU, boil)

- 1 oz. Hallertauer or Hersbrucker (3 HBU finish)

- 1 ½ oz. crushed coriander

- ½ oz. dried orange peel

- Belgian ale yeast

India Pale Ale

Ingredients:

- 6 lbs. Northwestern Pale liquid extract

- 1 lb. Lagglander Pale dry extract

- ½ lb. Crystal 40 L

- ½ lb. Toasted 25 L

- 3 oz. Cascade (whole leaf) 5.5% bitter

- 1 oz. Cascade (whole leaf) aroma

- 1 tsp. gypsum

- 1 tsp. Irish moss

- London yeast

ESB - Bitter Ale

Ingredients:

- 1 lb. Crystal 60 L

- 8 lb. amber liquid malt extract

- 1 oz. Northern Brewer hops bitter

- 1 oz. Yakima Goldings (add 30 minutes in boil flavoring hops)

- 1 oz. Yakima Goldings Aroma

- WLP-026 (White Labs liquid yeast: Bitter Ale) or similar

Brown Ale

Ingredients:

- 6 lb. light liquid malt extract

- 1 lb. crystal malt 60L

- 2 oz. Fuggles hops 3.6% AA bitter

- 1 oz. Willamette hops 4.3% AA aroma

- 5 gal. bottled drinking water

- ½ tsp. non-ionized salt

- 1 packet Nottingham Dry ale yeast

Bock

Ingredients:

- 4 lb. Laaglander Dutch Bock hopped malt extract

- 3.3 lb. Bierkeller dark malt extract

- ½ oz. Tettnanger hops (4.3% AA) flavor, last 15 minutes of boil

- ½ oz. Tettnanger hops aroma, added at end of boil

- Wyeast 1007 German ale yeast

Irish stout

Ingredients:

- 6.6 lbs John Bull Un-hopped dark malt extract

- ½ lb. Roasted unmalted barley

- ½ lb. Black Patent malt

- ⅓ oz. Burton Water Salts

- 3 oz. Cluster pellets (60 min. boil)

- 6 gal. water

- 1 pkg. Irish ale yeast

Bitter Dandelion

Ingredients:

- ½ lb. toasted malt

- ½ lb. 60 L British crystal malt

- 3.75 lbs. Cooper's Bitter Kit (You can buy this from many home-brew shops)

- 2 lbs. Munton and Fison Light DME

- 1 lb. dandelions (leaves, yellow blossoms and roots) You must clean and rinse these well before using.

- 1 oz. East Kent Goldings hops (flavor)

- ½ oz. Williamette hops (flavor)

- ½ oz. Williamette hops (aroma)

- London ale yeast

Bitter Quinoa

Ingredients:

- ½ lb. toasted malt

- ⅓ lb. biscuit malt

- ¼ lb. aromatic malt

- ½ lb. raw quinoa

- 4 lbs. Alexander's malt extract syrup

- 1 ½ lbs. Dutch extra dry DME

- 1 oz. East Kent Goldings (bitter)

- ½ oz. East Kent Goldings (flavoring)

- 1 oz. Williamette hops (flavoring)

- ½ oz. Williamette hops (aroma)

- 1 pkg. London ale yeast

Heather Ale

Ingredients:

- ¼ lb. toasted malt
- ⅓ lb. biscuit malt
- ⅓ lb. crystal malt
- ¼ lb. Special B malt
- 4 lbs. Geordie Scottish Export beer kit
- 2 lbs. light dry malt extract
- 12 c. dried heather blossoms
- Scottish ale yeast

Appendix A

Home-brew Journal

One way to keep up with your home-brew recipes and to record your successes and failures is to create a home-brew journal. You can buy journals at a bookstore, but it is just as easy to copy the next page and make one of your own. You can even create a virtual version that you can keep on your computer. You can paste a copy of the label on the page.

Name of beer: _____

Rating of this beer (scale 1-10, 1 being worst ever, 10 being best): ___

Date it was begun: _____

OG: _____

Yeast type: _____

FG: _____

Ingredients:

Instructions:

Hydrometer readings:

Date _____   Reading _____

Temperature readings:

Date _____   Reading _____

Acid readings:

Date _____   Reading _____

Hydrogen sulfite reading:

Date _____   Reading _____

PH reading:

Date _____   Reading _____

Notes:

Problems:

How I fixed it:

Changes in future batches:

Reviews of beer:

Date was first tasted:

Where it was first tasted:

This is just a template; you can be as creative as you want to be. However, you may want to take some steps to water-proof your journal. You can wrap it in food wrap or place it in a plastic zipper bag when you are using it on home brew days. You can also use a cookbook stand. If you are using a virtual version on your laptop, you can buy screen protectors and keyboard protectors. You can also place your laptop in an extra-large plastic bag and put a rubber band around it to make it snugger.

You can add some photos of your home-brew process and even photos of you and your friends drinking the home brew. A journal can be fun to create, but it can also contain all of your important home-brew recipes and secrets.

Resources for Home Brewing and Garden Supplies

This is an alphabetical listing of suppliers of home-brew equipment and gardening materials for growing herbs, grains, and hops at home.

Seeds

Some of the resources listed here are membership companies, like Seed Savers Exchange. The membership is not expensive and gives you a resource for some good heirloom varieties of plants. These organizations are dedicated to preserving the varieties that might otherwise disappear.

Abundant Life Seed Company
P.O. Box 279
Cottage Grove, OR 97424-0010
Phone: 541-767-9606
Fax: 866-514-7333
www.abundantlifeseeds.com

Bountiful Gardens
18001 Shafer Ranch Road
Willits, CA 95490
Phone: 707-459-6410
Fax: 707-459-1925
E-mail: bountiful@sonic.net
www.bountifulgardens.org

Fedco Seeds
P.O. Box 520
Waterville, ME 04903
Phone: 207-873-7333
www.fedcoseeds.com

Irish Eyes Garden Seeds
Phone: 509-933-7150
www.irisheyesgardenseeds.com

J.L. Hudson, Seedsman
P.O. Box 337
La Honda, California 94020
E-mail: inquiry@jlhudsonseeds.net
www.jlhudsonseeds.net

Johnny's Selected Seeds
955 Benton Ave.
Winslow, ME 04901
Phone: 877-564-6697
Fax: 800-738-6314
www.johnnyseeds.com

Pinetree Garden Seeds

P.O. Box 300
New Gloucester, ME 04260
Phone: 207-926-3400
Fax: 888-527-3337
E-mail: pinetree@superseeds.com
www.superseeds.com

R.H. Shumway's
334 W. Stroud St.
Randolph, WI 53956
Phone: 800-342-9461
www.rhshumway.com

Seeds of Change
Phone: 888-762-7333
www.seedsofchange.com

Seed Savers Exchange
3094 North Winn Road
Decorah, IA 52101
Phone: 563-382-5990
Fax: 563-382-5872
www.seedsavers.org

Herbs (Plants)

Artistic Gardens & LE Jardin du Gourmet
P.O. Box 75
St. Johnsbury Center, VT 05863
Phone: 802-748-1446
Fax: 802-748-1446
E-mail: OrderDesk@artisticgardens.com

www.artisticgardens.com

Edible Landscaping
361 Spirit Ridge Lane
Afton, VA 22920
Phone: 800-524-4156
Fax: 434-361-1916
www.ediblelandscaping.com

Gurney's Seed & Nursery Co.
P.O. Box 4178
Greendale, IN 47025-4178
Phone: 513-354-1492
Fax: 513-354-1493
www.gurneys.com

Heaths & Heathers Nursery
502 E. Haskell Hill Road
Shelton, WA 98584-8429
Phone: 360-427-5318
Fax: 800-294-3284
E-mail: handh@heathsandheathers.com
www.heathsandheathers.com

Henry Field's Seed & Nursery
P.O. Box 397
Aurora, IN 47001-0397
Phone: 513-354-1495
Fax: 513-354-1496
www.henryfields.com

JW Jung Quality Seeds

335 S. High St.
Randolph, WI 53956
Phone: 800-297-3123
www.jungseed.com

Richters Herbs
357 Highway 47
Goodwood, ON L0C 1A0 Canada
Phone: 905-640-6677
Fax: 905-640-6641
www.richters.com

Grain Seeds

Rupp Seeds, Inc.
17919 County Road B
Wauseon, OH 43567-9458
Phone: 419-337-1841
Fax: 419-337-5491
www.ruppseeds.com

Sustainable Seed Company
P.O. Box 636
Petaluma, CA 94952
Phone: 707-703-1242
www.sustainableseedco.com

Hop Rhizomes
Beer and WineMakers of America
755 E. Brokaw Road
San Jose, CA 95112
Phone: 408-441-0880

E-mail: BeerRich@yahoo.com
www.beerandwinemakers.com

Freshops
36180 Kings Valley Highway
Philomath, OR 97370
Phone: 541-929-2736
Fax: 541-929-2702
www.freshops.com

Nichols Garden Nursery
1190 Old Salem Road N.E.
Albany, OR 97321
Phone: 800-422-3985
Fax: 800-231-5306
www.nicholsgardennursery.com

Tools for the Garden

A.M. Leonard Tools
241 Fox Drive
P.O. Box 816
Piqua, OH 45356-0816
Phone: 800-543-8955
E-mail: info@amleo.com
www.AMLeo.com

Alternative Garden Supply
615 Industrial Drive
Cary, IL 60013
Phone: 847-516-4776

www.altgarden.com

Gempler's
P.O. Box 44993
Madison, WI 53744-4993
Phone: 800-382-8473
E-mail: customerservice@gemplers.com
www.gemplers.com

Kinsman Company
P.O. Box 428
Pipersville, PN 18947
Phone: 800-733.4146
Fax: 215-766-5624
E-mail: kinsco@kinsmangarden.com
www.kinsmangarden.com

Worm's Way
7854 North State Road 37
Bloomington, IN 47404
Sales: 800-274-9676
Fax: 800-466-0795
E-mail: info@wormsway.com
www.wormsway.com

Homebrew Suppliers
Austin Homebrew Supply
9129 Metric Blvd.
Austin, TX 78757
Phone: 800-890-2739
E-mail: info@austinhomebrew.com

www.austinhomebrew.com

Bacchus and Barleycorn Ltd.
6633 Nieman Road
Shawnee, KS 66203
Phone: 913-962-2501
Fax: 913-962-0008
www.bacchus-barleycorn.com

Beer and Wine Hobby
155 New Boston St.
Woburn, MA 01801-6297
Phone: 781-933-8818
www.beer-wine.com

The Beverage People
840 Piner Road
Santa Rosa, CA 95403
Phone: 800-544-1867
E-mail: info@thebeveragepeople.com
www.thebeveragepeople.com

Country Wines
3333 Babcock Boulevard
Pittsburgh, PA 15237-2421
Phone: 412-366-0151
www.countrywines.com/

Defalco's
8715 Stella Link Road
Houston, TX 77025-3401
Phone: 800-216-2739

Fax: 713-668-8856
E-mail: sales@defalcos.com
www.defalcos.com

E.C. Kraus
733 S. Northern Blvd.
P.O. Box 7850
Independence MO 64054
Phone: 800-353-1906
Fax: 816-254-7051
E-mail: customerservice@eckraus.com
www.eckraus.com

Grape and Granary
915 Home Ave.
Akron, OH 44310-4100
Phone: 800-695-9870
E-mail: info@grapeandgranary.com
www.grapeandgranary.com

Advantage Beer and Wine
2508-D Highway 70 S.W.
Hickory, NC 28602
Phone: 828-328-8140
www.hickorybrewer.com

Homebrew Adventures
1500 River Drive
Belmont, NC 28012
Phone: 800-365-2739
http://ebrew.com

The Homebrewery
205 West Bain
P.O. Box 730
Ozark, MO 65721
Phone: 800-321-2739
Fax: 417-485-4107
E-mail: brewery@homebrewery.com
www.homebrewery.com/

Just Brew It!
1855 Cassat Ave. No. 5B
Jacksonville, FL 32210
Phone: 904-381-1983
E-mail: info@justbrewitjax.com
www.justbrewitjax.com

Midwest Homebrewing Supplies
3440 Belt Line Blvd.
Minneapolis, MN 55416
Phone: 888-449-2739
Fax: 952-925-9867
www.midwestsupplies.com

Princeton Homebrew
208 Sanhican Drive
Trenton, NJ 08542
Phone: 609-252-1800

Seven Bridges Cooperative
325A River St.
Santa Cruz, CA 95060

Phone: 800-768-4409

E-mail: 7bridges@breworganic.com

www.breworganic.com

William's Brewing Company

2088 Burroughs Ave.

San Leandro, CA 94577

Phone: 800-759-6025

E-mail: service@williamsbrewing.com

www.williamsbrewing.com

Windriver Brewing Company

861 10th Ave.

Barron, WI 54812

Phone: 800-266-4677

E-mail: windrvr@bitstream.net

www.windriverbrew.com

Northwest Hops

Phone: 559-212-4677

E-mail: Sales@northwesthops.com

www.northwesthops.com

The Drip Store

160 Highway 70 West

Havelock, NC 28532

Phone: 252-463-3747

Toll Free: 877-858-4015

Fax: 252-463-3501

www.dripirrigation.com

Live Beneficial Insects

Arbico Organics
P.O. Box 8910
Tucson, AZ
Phone: 800-827-2847
www.arbico-organics.com

Growquest
134 Davis St.
Santa Paula, CA 93060
Phone: 805-921-3900
www.growquest.com

Gardens Alive
5100 Schenley Place
Lawrenceburg, IN 47025
Phone: 513-354-1482
www.gardensalive.com

Bug Blaster
P.O. Box 73125
San Clemente, CA 92673
Phone: 949-493-3310
Fax: 949-388-0279
E-mail: thebugblaster@cox.net
www.thebugblaster.com

Yeast Suppliers

Wyeast Laboratories, Inc.
P.O. Box 146

Odell, OR 97044
www.wyeastlab.com

Whitelabs
5455 Spine Road, Mezzanine East
Boulder, CO 80301
Phone: 303-530-0469
Fax: 888-693-1026 (U.S. & Canada only)
www.whitelabs.com

Appendix C

List of Yeast Strains

White Labs and Wyeast are the two main suppliers of beer yeast. In this Appendix is a list of the different types of yeast that White Labs offers. Yeast can be purchased from the company. Many beer supply companies also carry this brand of yeast.

Alcohol tolerance refers to how high the potential alcohol level a beer would be using a particular yeast. It refers to how tolerant the beer yeast is and at what level they would begin to die from alcohol poisoning. Here is a reference to how high the potential alcohol would be in a beer as compared to its alcohol tolerance.

Very high: over 15 percent
High: 10 to 15 percent
Medium-high: 8 to 12 percent
Medium: 5 to 10 percent
Low: 2 to 5 percent

You will also notice the temperature at which the yeast will ferment. These are the target temperatures at which your yeast will ferment the best. Some yeast does not work at all under certain temperatures, and these are noted in the chart.

Two other terms are important when reading this chart: attenuation and flocculation.

Attenuation

Yeast is responsible for turning sweet wort into what we call "beer." Yeast consumes the sugar in wort and turns that sugar into CO_2, alcohol, and flavor compounds. When yeast finishes the fermentation process, it shuts down, clumps together, and falls to the bottom of the fermenter, or "flocculates." When yeast flocculates, it is easy to see that fermentation is done. But how can the brewer be sure? What if the flocculation is minimal, and the yeast and CO_2 stay in solution? How does the brewer really know when fermentation is done? The answer: by testing the degree of attenuation. Apparent attenuation percentage is the percentage of sugars that yeast consumes. Attenuation varies between different strains. The fermentation conditions and gravity of a particular beer will cause the attenuation to vary, hence, the reason each strain of brewer's yeast has a characteristic attenuation range. The range for brewer's yeast is typically between 65 to 85 percent.

How does a brewer calculate attenuation? First, the specific gravity must be checked with a hydrometer before the yeast is pitched. Specific gravity is a measurement of density. The specific gravity of water is 1.000, and wort has a higher density relative to water because of the sugars present in wort. As these sugars are consumed by yeast during fermentation, the density — and therefore the SG measurement — lowers. The yeast also produces alcohol, which is lighter than water, so to obtain the "actual" attenuation, alcohol must be removed by heat and replaced by water. Only large breweries go to such lengths to report the "actual" attenuation, while the attenuation most home brewers measure is "apparent" attenuation. The specific gravity measured before pitching, after correcting for temperature — the OG — needs to be logged into a brewer's notebook. Then, during fermentation, the SG can be re-checked. The specific gravity will fall toward 1.000 during fermentation, and a brewer can learn much about the fermentation by checking the specific gravity of the beer daily. Once the gravity remains the same for three days in a row, the yeast is most likely done with fermentation. To calculate attenuation percentage, the following equation can be used:

$$[(OG-FG)/(OG-1)] \times 100$$

The only way to know if yeast has completed fermentation is to check the expected attenuation. Many home brewers make the mistake of worrying about a beer before they even check the attenuation. A simple check of the specific gravity at the end of fermentation will help in this regard. It is not completely accurate without computing the attenuation. For example, if a high gravity beer is made, the FG will be higher then normal, but the expected attenuation for that yeast strain may have been obtained. *To obtain expected attenuation numbers, consult the yeast strain attenuation figures later in this Appendix.*

Most manufactures of brewer's yeast list the attenuation ranges of their yeast strains. This can be very useful to a brewer in matching a yeast strain to a beer style. An example would be a brewer who wishes to make American-style pale ale. A yeast strain should be selected that will produce a dry finish and allow hop flavors to come through. A good choice would be neutral yeast with an attenuation of 70 to 80 percent. If a brewer wants to make English-style mild ale, a yeast strain that does not attenuate as much would be desired. An attenuation range of 65 to 70 percent would be more appropriate. Would a yeast strain that attenuates to 80 percent taste bad in English-style mild ale? No, but the beer would not taste true to style.

Flocculation

Brewers have created their own unique vocabulary. Words such as pitching, attenuation, and flocculation take on special meaning to brewers. Pitching is adding yeast to wort to start fermentation. Attenuation is the percentage of sugars yeast consume during fermentation. The magical art of yeast coming together and dropping to the bottom of a fermenter is called flocculation.

Flocculation is a desirable and important characteristic that is unique to brewer's yeast. When brewer's yeast nears the end of fermentation, single cells aggregate into clumps of thousands of cells and drop to the bottom of the fermenter, leaving clear beer behind. If yeast flocculates too early, the beer will be under-attenuated and sweet. If yeast does not flocculate, the beer will be cloudy and have a yeasty taste.

Most strains of yeast, which brewers call wild yeast, do not flocculate well and remain in suspension for extended periods. The ability to flocculate is a product of natural selection. Brewers have continually collected yeast either from the bottom or top of a fermenter, and in doing so, have selected for increasingly flocculent strains. The chemistry of flocculation is complex, but having a basic understanding will suffice for the home brewer.

Yeast flocculation can be classified as high, medium, or low. Ale yeast strains are found in each category, while lager yeast are predominantly medium flocculators. An English/London ale strain would be a high flocculator, while a California/American ale strain would be a medium flocculator. A Hefeweizen strain is an example of a low flocculator. It is difficult to tell which category of flocculator is used to produce individual commercial beers, because most commercial beers are filtered before being bottled or kegged.

Ale yeast

Yeast Name	Description	Attenuation	Flocculation	Optimum Fermentation Temperature	Alcohol Tolerance
WLP001 California Ale Yeast	This yeast is famous for its clean flavors, balance, and ability to be used in almost any style ale. It accentuates the hop flavors and is extremely versatile.	73-80%	Medium	68-73° F (20-23° C)	High
WLP002 English Ale Yeast	A classic ESB strain from one of England's largest independent breweries, this yeast is best suited for English style ales, including milds, bitters, porters, and English-style stouts. This yeast will leave a beer very clear and will leave some residual sweetness.	63-70%	High	65-68° F (18-20° C)	Medium
WLP004 Irish Ale Yeast	This is the yeast from one of the oldest stout producing breweries in the world. It produces a slight hint of diacetyl, balanced by a light fruitiness and slight, dry crispness. Great for Irish ales, stouts, porters, browns, reds, and a very interesting pale ale.	69-74%	Medium to high	65-68° F (18-20° C)	Medium-high

Yeast Name	Description	Attenuation	Flocculation	Optimum Fermentation Temperature	Alcohol Tolerance
WLP005 British Ale Yeast	*This yeast is a little more attenuative than WLP002. Like most English strains, this yeast produces malty beers. Excellent for all English-style ales, including bitter, pale ale, porter, and brown ale.*	*67-74%*	*High*	*65-70° F (18-21° C)*	*Medium*
WLP006 Bedford British	*Ferments dry and flocculates very well. Produces a distinctive ester profile. Good choice for most English-style ales, including bitter, pale ale, porter, and brown ale.*	*72-80%*	*High*	*65-70° F (18-21° C)*	*Medium*
WLP007 Dry English Ale Yeast	*Clean, highly flocculent, and highly attenuative yeast. This yeast is similar to WLP002 in flavor profile, but is 10 percent more attenuative. This eliminates the residual sweetness and makes the yeast well suited for high-gravity ales. It is also reaches terminal gravity quickly. Eighty percent attenuation will be reached even with 10-percent ABV beers.*	*70-80%*	*Medium to high*	*65-70° F (18-21° C)*	*Medium-high*

Yeast Name	Description	Attenuation	Flocculation	Optimum Fermentation Temperature	Alcohol Tolerance
WLP008 East Coast Ale Yeast	Strain can be used to reproduce many of the American versions of classic beer styles. Similar neutral character of WLP001, but less attenuation, less accentuation of hop bitterness, slightly less flocculation, and a little tartness. Very clean and low esters. Great yeast for golden, blond, honey, pales, and German alt-style ales.	70-75%	Medium to low	68-73° F (20-23° C)	Medium
WLP009 Australian Ale Yeast	Produces a clean, malty beer. Pleasant ester character can be described as "bready." Can ferment successfully and clean at higher temperatures. This yeast combines good flocculation with good attenuation.	70-75%	High	65-70° F (18-21° C)	Medium
WLP011 European Ale Yeast	Malty, northern European-origin ale yeast. Low ester production, giving a clean profile. Little to no sulfur production. Low attenuation helps to contribute to the malty character. Good for Alt, Kölsch, malty English ales, and fruit beers.	65-70%	Medium	65-70° F (18-21° C)	Medium

Yeast Name	Description	Attenuation	Flocculation	Optimum Fermentation Temperature	Alcohol Tolerance
WLP013 London Ale Yeast	*Dry, malty ale yeast. Provides a complex, oaky ester character to your beer. Hop bitterness comes through well. This yeast is well suited for classic British pale ales, bitters, and stouts. Does not flocculate as much as WLP002 and WLP005.*	*67-75%*	*Medium*	*66-71° F (19-22° C)*	*Medium*
WLP022 Essex Ale Yeast	*Flavorful British style yeast. Drier finish than many British ale yeasts. Produces slightly fruity and bready character. Good top fermenting yeast strain, well suited for top cropping (collecting). This yeast is well suited for classic British milds, pale ales, bitters, and stouts. Does not flocculate as much as WLP002 and WLP005.*	*71-76%*	*Medium to high*	*66-70° F (19-21° C)*	*Medium*

Yeast Name	Description	Attenuation	Flocculation	Optimum Fermentation Temperature	Alcohol Tolerance
WLP023 Burton Ale Yeast	From the famous brewing town of Burton upon Trent, England, this yeast is packed with character. It provides delicious, subtle, fruity flavors like apple, clover honey, and pear. Great for all English styles, IPAs, bitters, and pales. Excellent in porters and stouts.	69-75%	Medium	68-73° F (20-23° C)	Medium
WLP028 Edinburgh Scottish Ale Yeast	Scotland is famous for its malty, strong ales. This yeast can reproduce complex, flavorful Scottish-style ales. This yeast can be an everyday strain, similar to WLP001. Hop character is not muted with this strain, as it is with WLP002.	70-75%	Medium	65-70 F (18-21° C) Does not ferment well less than 62° F (17° C)	Medium-high
WLP029 German Ale/Kölsch Yeast	From a small brewpub in Cologne, Germany, this yeast works great in Kölsch and Alt-style beers. Good for light beers like blond and honey. Accentuates hop flavors similar to WLP001. Slight sulfur produced during fermentation will disappear with age and leave a super clean, lager-like ale.	72-78%	Medium	65-69° F (18-21° C) Does not ferment well less than 62° F (17° C), unless during active fermentation	Medium

Yeast Name	Description	Attenuation	Flocculation	Optimum Fermentation Temperature	Alcohol Tolerance
WLP036 Dusseldorf Alt Yeast	*Traditional Alt yeast from Dusseldorf, Germany. Produces clean, slightly sweet alt beers. Does not accentuate hop flavor as WLP029 does.*	*65-72%*	*Medium*	*65-69° F (18-21° C)*	*Medium*
WLP037 Yorkshire Square Ale Yeast	*This yeast produces a beer that is malty, but well balanced. Expect flavors that are toasty with malt-driven esters. Highly flocculent and good choice for English pale ales, English brown ales, and mild ales.*	*68-72%*	*High*	*65-69° F (18-21° C)*	*Medium-high*
WLP038 Manchester Ale Yeast	*Top-fermenting strain that is traditionally good for top cropping. Moderately flocculent with a clean, dry finish. Low ester profile, producing a highly balanced English-style beer.*	*70-74%*	*Medium-high*	*65-70° F (18-21° C)*	*Medium-high*
WLP039 Nottingham Ale Yeast	*British-style ale yeast with a very dry finish. Medium to low fruit and fusel alcohol production. Good top-fermenting yeast strain, well suited for top cropping (collecting). This yeast is well suited for pale ales, ambers, porters, and stouts.*	*73-82%*	*Medium to high*	*66-70° F (19-21° C)*	*Medium*

Yeast Name	Description	Attenuation	Flocculation	Optimum Fermentation Temperature	Alcohol Tolerance
WLP041 Pacific Ale Yeast	*Popular ale yeast from the Pacific Northwest. The yeast will clear from the beer well, and leave a malty profile. More fruity than WLP002, English Ale Yeast. Good yeast for English-style ales, including milds, bitters, IPA, porters, and English-style stouts.*	*65-70%*	*High*	*65-68° F (18-20° C)*	*Medium*
WLP051 California Ale V Yeast	*From Northern California. This strain is fruitier than WLP001, and slightly more flocculent. Attenuation is lower, resulting in a fuller-bodied beer than with WLP001.*	*70-75%*	*Medium to high*	*66-70° F (19-21° C)*	*Medium-high*

Yeast Name	Description	Attenuation	Flocculation	Optimum Fermentation Temperature	Alcohol Tolerance
WLP060 American Ale Yeast Blend	*Our most popular yeast strain is WLP001, California Ale Yeast. This blend celebrates the strengths of California – clean, neutral fermentation, versatile usage and adds two other strains that belong to the same "clean/neutral" flavor category. The additional strains create complexity to the finished beer. This blend tastes more lager-like than WLP001. Hop flavors and bitterness are accentuated, but not to the extreme of California. Slight sulfur will be produced during fermentation.*	*72-80%*	*Medium*	*68-72° F (20-22° C)*	*Medium high*
WLP072 French Ale	*Clean strain that complements malt flavor. Low to moderate esters, when fermentation temperature is below 70° F. Moderate plus ester character over 70° F. Low diacetyl production. Good yeast strain for Biere de Garde, blond, amber, brown ales, and specialty beers*	*68-75%*	*Medium high*	*63-73° F (17-23° C)*	*Medium high*

Yeast Name	Description	Attenuation	Flocculation	Optimum Fermentation Temperature	Alcohol Tolerance
WLP080 Cream Ale Yeast Blend	This is a blend of ale and lager yeast strains. The strains work together to create a clean, crisp, light American lager-style ale. A pleasing ester-like aroma may be perceived from the ale yeast contribution. Hop flavors and bitterness are slightly subdued. Slight sulfur will be produced during fermentation, from the lager yeast.	75-80%	Medium	65-70° F (18-21° C)	Medium high
WLP099 Super High Gravity Ale Yeast	Can ferment up to 25 percent alcohol. From England. Produces ester character that increases with increasing gravity. Malt character dominates at lower gravities.	>80%	Medium	65-69° F (18-21° C)	Very high

Specialty/Belgian yeast

Yeast Name	Description	Attenuation	Flocculation	Optimum Fermentation Temperature	Alcohol Tolerance
WLP300 Hefeweizen Ale Yeast	*This famous German yeast is a strain used in the production of traditional, authentic wheat beers. It produces the banana and clove nose traditionally associated with German wheat beers and leaves the desired cloudy look of traditional German wheat beers.*	*72-76%*	*Low*	*68-72° F (20-22° C)*	*Medium*
WLP320 American Hefeweizen Ale Yeast	*This yeast is used to produce the Oregon-style American Hefeweizen. Unlike WLP300, this yeast produces a very slight amount of the banana and clove notes. It produces some sulfur, but is otherwise a clean fermenting yeast, which does not flocculate well, producing a cloudy beer.*	*70-75%*	*Low*	*65-69° F (18-21° C)*	*Medium*

Yeast Name	Description	Attenuation	Flocculation	Optimum Fermentation Temperature	Alcohol Tolerance
WLP351 Bavarian Weizen Yeast	Former Yeast Lab W51 yeast strain, acquired from Dan McConnell. The description originally used by Yeast Lab still fits: "This strain produces a classic German-style wheat beer, with moderately high, spicy, phenolic overtones reminiscent of cloves."	73-77%	Low	66-70° F (19-21° C)	Medium
WLP380 Hefeweizen IV Ale Yeast	Large clove and phenolic aroma and flavor, with minimal banana. Refreshing citrus and apricot notes. Crisp, drinkable hefeweizen. Less flocculent than WLP300, and sulfur production is higher.	73-80%	Low	66-70° F (19-21° C)	Medium
WLP400 Belgian Wit Ale Yeast	Slightly phenolic and tart, this is the original yeast used to produce Wit in Belgium.	74-78%	Low to medium	67-74° F (19-23° C)	Medium

Yeast Name	Description	Attenuation	Flocculation	Optimum Fermentation Temperature	Alcohol Tolerance
WLP410 Belgian Wit II Ale Yeast	*Less phenolic than WLP400, and spicier. Will leave a bit more sweetness; flocculation is higher than WLP400. Use to produce Belgian Wit, spiced Ales, wheat ales, and specialty beers.*	*70-75%*	*Low to medium*	*67-74° F (19-23° C)*	*Medium*
WLP500 Trappist Ale Yeast	*From one of the few Trappist breweries remaining in the world, this yeast produces the distinctive fruitiness and plum characteristics. Excellent yeast for high gravity beers, Belgian ales, dubbels, and trippels.*	*75-80%*	*Medium to low*	*65-72° F (18-22° C) Lower temperatures (under 65° F (18° C) will result in earthier, less fruity, beers.*	*High*
WLP510 Belgian Bastogne Ale Yeast	*A high gravity, Trappist-style ale yeast. Produces dry beer with slight acidic finish. More "clean" fermentation character than WLP500 or WLP530. Not as spicy as WLP530 or WLP550. Excellent yeast for high-gravity beers, Belgian ales, dubbels, and trippels.*	*74-80%*	*High*	*66-72° F (19-22° C)*	*Medium*

Yeast Name	Description	Attenuation	Flocculation	Optimum Fermentation Temperature	Alcohol Tolerance
WLP515 Antwerp Ale Yeast	Clean, almost lager-like, Belgian-type ale yeast. Good for Belgian-type pales ales and amber ales, or with blends to combine with other Belgian-type yeast strains. Biscuity, ale-like aroma present. Hop flavors and bitterness are accentuated. Slight sulfur will be produced during fermentation, which can give the yeast a lager-like flavor profile.	73-80%	Medium	67-70°F (19-21° C)	Medium
WLP530 Abbey Ale Yeast	Used to produce Trappist-style beers. Similar to WLP500, but is less fruity and more alcohol-tolerant (up to 15% ABV). Excellent yeast for high-gravity beers, Belgian ales, dubbels, and trippels.	75-80%	Medium to high	66-72° F (19-22° C)	High
WLP540 Abbey IV Ale Yeast	Authentic Trappist-style yeast. Use for Belgian style ales, dubbels, trippels, and specialty beers. Fruit character is medium, in between WLP500 (high) and WLP530 (low).	74-82%	Medium	66-72° F (19-22° C)	High

Yeast Name	Description	Attenuation	Flocculation	Optimum Fermentation Temperature	Alcohol Tolerance
WLP545 Belgian Strong Ale Yeast	From the Ardennes region of Belgium, this classic yeast strain produces moderate levels of ester and spicy phenolic character. Typically results in a dry, but balanced, finish. This yeast is well suited for Belgian dark strongs, Abbey Ales, and Christmas beers.	78-85%	Medium	66-72° F (19-22° C)	High
WLP550 Belgian Ale Yeast	Saisons, Belgian ales, Belgian reds, Belgian browns, and white beers are just a few of the classic Belgian beer styles that can be created with this yeast strain. Phenolic and spicy flavors dominate the profile, with less fruitiness then WLP500.	78-85%	Medium	68-78° F (20-26° C)	Medium-high
WLP565 Belgian Saison I Yeast	Classic Saison yeast from Wallonia. It produces earthy, peppery, and spicy notes. Slightly sweet. With high-gravity Saisons, brewers may wish to dry the beer with an alternate yeast added after 75 percent fermentation.	65-75%	Medium	68-75° F (20-24° C)	Medium

Yeast Name	Description	Attenuation	Flocculation	Optimum Fermentation Temperature	Alcohol Tolerance
WLP566 Belgian Saison II Yeast	Saison strain with fruitier ester production than with WLP565. Moderately phenolic, with a clove-like characteristic in finished beer flavor and aroma. Ferments faster than WLP565.	78-85%	Medium	68-78° F (20-26° C)	Medium
WLP568 Belgian Style Saison Ale Yeast Blend	This blend melds Belgian-style ale and Saison strains. The strains work in harmony to create complex fruity aromas and flavors. The blend of yeast strains encourages complete fermentation in a timely manner. Phenolic, spicy, earthy, and clove-like flavors are also created.	70-80%	Medium	70-80° F (21-27° C)	Medium
WLP570 Belgian Golden Ale Yeast	From East Flanders, versatile yeast that can produce light Belgian ales to high gravity Belgian beers (12% ABV). A combination of fruitiness and phenolic characteristics dominate the flavor profile. Sulfur produced during fermentation will dissipate following the end of fermentation.	73-78%	Low	68-75° F (20-24° C)	High

Yeast Name	Description	Attenuation	Flocculation	Optimum Fermentation Temperature	Alcohol Tolerance
WLP575 Belgian Style Ale Yeast Blend	*A blend of Trappist-type yeast (2) and one Belgian ale-type yeast. This creates a versatile blend that can be used for Trappist-type beer, or myriad beers that can be described as "Belgian type."*	*74-80%*	*Medium*	*68-75° F (20-24° C)*	*Medium-high*

Lager yeast

Yeast Name	Description	Attenuation	Flocculation	Optimum Fermentation Temperature	Alcohol Tolerance
WLP800 Pilsner Lager Yeast	*Classic pilsner strain from the premier pilsner producer in the Czech Republic. Somewhat dry with a malty finish, this yeast is best suited for European pilsner production.*	*72-77%*	*Medium to high*	*50-55° F (10-13° C)*	*Medium*

Yeast Name	Description	Attenuation	Flocculation	Optimum Fermentation Temperature	Alcohol Tolerance
WLP802 Czech Budejovice Lager Yeast	Pilsner lager yeast from Southern Czech Republic. Produces dry and crisp lagers, with low diacetyl production.	75-80%	Medium	50-55° F (10-13° C)	Medium
WLP810 San Francisco Lager Yeast	This yeast is used to produce the "California Common"-style beer. A unique lager strain that has the ability to ferment up to 65° F while retaining lager characteristics. Can also be fermented down to 50° F for production of marzens, pilsners, and other style lagers.	65-70%	High	58-65° F (14-18° C)	Medium-high
WLP820 Oktoberfest/ Märzen Lager Yeast	This yeast produces a very malty, bock-like style. It does not finish as dry as WLP830. This yeast is much slower in the first generation than WLP830, so we encourage use of a larger starter the first generation, or schedule a longer lagering time.	65-73%	Medium	52-58° F (11-14° C)	Medium-high

Yeast Name	Description	Attenuation	Flocculation	Optimum Fermentation Temperature	Alcohol Tolerance
WLP830 German Lager Yeast	*This yeast is one of the most widely used lager yeasts in the world. Very malty and clean, great for all German lagers, Pilsner, Oktoberfest, and Marzen.*	*74-79%*	*Medium*	*50-55° F (10-13° C)*	*Medium*
WLP833 German Bock Lager Yeast	*From the Alps of southern Bavaria, this yeast produces a beer that is well balanced between malt and hop character. The excellent malt profile makes it well suited for Bocks, Doppelbocks, and Oktoberfest-style beers. Very versatile lager yeast, it is so well balanced that it has gained tremendous popularity for use in Classic American-style Pilsners. Also good for Helles-style lager beer.*	*70-76%*	*Medium*	*48-55° F (9-13° C)*	*Medium-high*

Yeast Name	Description	Attenuation	Flocculation	Optimum Fermentation Temperature	Alcohol Tolerance
WLP838 Southern German Lager Yeast	This yeast is characterized by a malty finish and balanced aroma. It is a strong fermenter, producing slight sulfur and low diacetyl.	68-76%	Medium to high	50-55° F (10-13° C)	Medium
WLP840 American Lager Yeast	This yeast is used to produce American-style lagers. Dry and clean with a very slight apple fruitiness. Sulfur and diacetyl production is minimal.	75-80%	Medium	50-55° F (10-13° C)	
WLP850 Copenhagen Lager Yeast	Clean, crisp north European lager yeast. Not as malty as the southern European lager yeast strains. Great for European-style pilsners, European-style dark, Vienna- and American-style lagers.	72-78%	Medium	50-58° F (10-14° C)	Medium

Yeast Name	Description	Attenuation	Flocculation	Optimum Fermentation Temperature	Alcohol Tolerance
WLP885 Zurich Lager Yeast	*Swiss-style lager yeast. With proper care, this yeast can be used to produce lager beer over 11 percent ABV. Sulfur and diacetyl production is minimal. Original culture provided to White Labs by Marc Sedam.*	*70-80%*	*Medium*	*50-55° F (10-13° C)*	*Very High*
WLP920 Old Bavarian Lager Yeast	*From Southern Germany, this yeast finishes malty with a slight ester profile. Use in beers such as Oktoberfest, Bock, and dark lagers.*	*66-73%*	*Medium*	*50-55° F (10-13° C)*	*Medium-high*
WLP940 Mexican Lager Yeast	*From Mexico City, this yeast produces clean lager beer, with a crisp finish. Good for Mexican-style light lagers, as well as dark lagers.*	*70-78%*	*Medium*	*50-55° F (10-13° C)*	*Medium*

Brettanomyces and Bacteria

WLP645 Brettanomyces claussenii

Low intensity Brett character. Originally isolated from strong, English-stock beer in the early 20th century. The Brett flavors produced are subtler than WLP650 and WLP653. More aroma than flavor contribution. Fruity, pineapple-like aroma. B. claussenii is closely related to B. anomalus.

WLP650 Brettanomyces bruxellensis

Medium-intensity Brett character. Classic strain used in secondary fermentation for Belgian-style beers and lambics. One Trappist brewery uses this strain in secondary fermentation and bottling to produce their characteristic flavor.

WLP653 Brettanomyces lambicus

High-intensity Brett character. Defines the "Brett character": horsey, smoky, and spicy flavors. As the name suggests, this strain is found most often in lambic-style beers, which are spontaneously fermented beers. Also found in Flanders and sour brown-style beers.

WLP655 Belgian Sour Mix 1

A unique blend perfect for Belgian-style beers. Includes Brettanomyces, Saccharomyces, and the bacterial strains Lactobacillus and Pediococcus.

WLP677 Lactobacillus Bacteria

Lactic acid bacteria produce moderate levels of acidity and sour flavors found in lambics, Berliner Weiss, sour brown ale, and Gueze.

Appendix D

Malt Types and Uses

In this Appendix are different common malts, their Lovibond numbers, and their common uses in beers. This is not a complete list because different breweries can produce their own special malts. The good news is that because you are growing your own grains at home, you can experiment and come up with specialty grains of your own.

Mashed Malts

Lager/Pilsner malt 2 degrees Lovibond. This is the base malt for just about every beer made. It can stand alone in a pale ale or be used a fermentable malt for about any other kind of beer. Usually, if there is the label pilsner malt, it is created from two-row barley.

Caramelized (crystal) malts

Name of crystal malt	Type of malt	Use
Carapils	Dextrin malt	The dextrin in this malt affects the mouth feel, body, and full taste of the beer. It also lends to foam stability. This malt must be mashed with pale malt because it lacks the necessary enzymes to break down the starch in them.
10 L crystal	caramel malt	This is a lot like carpils, but has a lighter caramel sweetness.
40 L crystal	caramel malt	This pale crystal malt will lend a balance of medium caramel color, flavor, and body.
60 L crystal	caramel malt	This has a well-balanced color, caramel flavor, and sweet taste.
80 L crystal	caramel malt	This has a more distinct flavor, color, and sweetness of caramel.
120 L crystal	caramel malt	This dark crystal malt offers a sharper and more complex caramel flavor and aroma. This is used as a specialty grain and in small amounts in most beers, but does well in larger amounts in heavier, stouter beers.
German	caramel malt	It is used in pilsner beers, as it adds body and balance to a beer.
Light crystal	20 L caramel	This type of German caramel malt adds a little more body to pilsners.
German medium crystal	50 L caramel	Another type of German caramel malt. This is used with lager-type beers to add body and sweetness.
German dark crystal	90-110 L caramel	This type of German caramel adds a strong body and caramel color. It is used in dark, lager-style beers.
English crystal	17 L caramel malt	This malt is also known as light CaraStan. This malt has a toffee-like, sweet flavor that is light in color.

Name of crystal malt	Type of malt	Use
English crystal	37 L caramel malt	This is also called CaraStan. This is used for pale ales and bitters and has a fuller toffee flavor.
English crystal	55 L caramel malt	This is used for dark ales.
English crystal	80 L caramel malt	The color this imparts is amber and has a stronger toffee flavor.
English crystal	140 L caramel malt	The color this imparts is a deep-red color. Has a caramelized and roasted flavor.
Scottish crystal	90 L caramel malt	The color of this malt is deep red to amber. It has a toasted-caramel flavor.
Belgian caravienne	22 L caramel	The aroma is sweet caramel and has a full flavor. This is a good overall caramel malt.
Belgian Caramünich	60 L caramel	This has a rich malt aroma and deep color.
Belgian special B	150-220 L caramel	This is one of the darkest crystal malts. Its caramelization is high, which imparts a nice, nutty flavor to the beer.

Bibliography

Davids, Kenneth. *Home Coffee Roasting*. New York: St. Martin's Griffin, 2003.

Myrick, Herbet. *The Hop; Its Culture and Cure, Marketing and Manufacture; a Practical Handbook on the Most Improved Methods in Growing, Harvesting, Curing and Selling Hops, and on the Use and Manufacture of Hops*. New York: Orange Judd, 1899.

Mahaffee, W.F.; Pethybridge, S.J.; and Gent, D.H. *Compendium of Hop Diseases and Pests*. Amer. Phyto. Soc. Press, 2009.

MacVannel, Alexander Peter. *Barley: Its Production and Uses with Special Reference to Malting and Brewing Qualities*. BiblioBazaar, 1908.

Calagione, Sam. *An Enthusiast's Guide to Brewing Craft Beer at Home: Extreme Brewing*. Quarry, 2006.

Nachel, Marty. *Homebrewing for Dummies*. 2nd ed. New Jersey: Wiley, 2008.

Higgins, Patrick, Kilgore, Maura Kate and Hertlein, Paul. *The Homebrewer's Recipe Guide: More than 175 original beer recipes, including magnificent pale ales, ambers, stouts, lagers, and seasonal brews, plus tips from the master brewers*. New York: Simon and Schuster, 1996.

Szamatulski, Tess and Mark. *Homebrew Recipes for 150 Commercial Beers: Clone Brews*. Maine: Storey, 1998.

Kania, Leon. *The Alaska Bootlegger's Bible: Makin' beer, wine, liqueurs and moonshine whiskey; and old Alaskan tell how it's done*. Alaska: Happy Mountain, 2000.

Pitzer, Sara. *Homegrown Whole Grains: Grow, Harvest & Cook Wheat, Barley, Oats, Rice, Corn & More*. Maine: Storey, 2009.

Logsdon, Gene. *Small- scale Grain Raising: An Organic Guide to Growing, Processing, and Using Nutritious Whole Grains for Home Gardeners and Local Farmers*. 2nd ed. Pennsylvania: Rodale, 2009.

Simmonds, P.L. *Hops; Their Cultivation, Commerce and Uses in Various Countries*. Bibliolife, 1877.

Fisher, Joe, Fisher, Dennis. *The Homebrewer's Garden: How to easily grow, prepare, and use your own hops, malts and brewing herbs*. Maine: Storey, 1998.

Palmer, John J. *How to Brew: Everything you need to know to brew right the first time.* Colorado: 2006.

Cherney, Y. and White, C. *The Fungus Among Us.* 3rd ed. Fermat-ap, 2008.

Hop Varieties
University of Vermont Extension System

Department of Plant and Soil Science

www.uvm.edu/~pass/perry/hopvars.html

More on Growing Hops
University of Vermont Extension System

Department of Plant and Soil Science

www.uvm.edu/~pass/perry/hopsmore.html

Guide to Growing Your Own Hops
Ratebeer Weekly Magazine

www.ratebeer.com/Story.asp?StoryID=186

How to Make Crystal Malts at Home
Home Brew Chatter Board

www.homebrewchatter.com/board/archive/index.
php/t-7233.html

Malt Varieties

The Foam Rangers Beer Club

www.foamrangers.com/malts.html

Basic Hop Growing Instruction Article

From growinghopsyourself.com

www.squidoo.com/growinghops

Starting your Hops from Rhizomes

Growing Hops Yourself

www.growinghopsyourself.com/growing-hops/growing-
hops-from-rhizomes

Disease Management for Barley

University of Vermont

www.ppws.vt.edu/stromberg/smallgrain/control/bcultivar.
html

Grain Amaranth A Lost Crop of the Americas

Thomas Jefferson Agricultural Institute

www.jeffersoninstitute.org/pubs/amaranth.shtml

Basic Instructions for using a Garden Hoe

From Gardenaction.co.uk

www.gardenaction.co.uk/weed_control/garden_hoe.asp

Common Corn Diseases

Center for Integrated Pest Management, NCSU

http://ipm.ncsu.edu/corn/diseases/corn_diseases.html

Eddleman, Harold. Sterilizing and Storing your Media, Using Your Autoclave (Pressure Cooker).

www.disknet.com/indiana_biolab/b024.htm

A

Acrospire. A plant shoot that grows from a seed.

Aeration. Dissolving oxygen into media, which is the material that yeast grows on, by shaking a container in an effort to help yeast growth. Also refers to adding oxygen to wort that is fermenting.

Aerobic. In the presence of oxygen. Yeast grows at a faster rate and undergoes cell development for healthy life in an oxygenated environment.

Agar. A seaweed product used to solidify wort media in slants and plates.

Aleurone layer. The outermost part of a grain.

Anaerobic. Devoid of oxygen. This phase forces the yeast in the fermentation cycle.

Anthracnose. A fungal disease that appears as small, either oval or elongated, water-soaked spots. These spots can appear at any time on the leaves of corn. As the disease progresses, these spots will grow together to affect the entire leaf and kill it.

Attenuation. The degree to which yeast is able to ferment the sugars present in the wort. The higher the attenuation, the dryer the finished beer will be (low terminal gravities). The lower the attenuation, the sweeter and maltier a beer will be (higher terminal gravities).

Autoclaved. Heated and steamed under pressure, killing all microbial life and rendering sterile.

Awn. Stiff bristle at the top of the plant.

B

Bacterial leaf blight. A corn plant infection that appears as pale green to yellow, irregular streaks in the leaves. As the disease progresses, the leaves die and dry up. This results in a small yield and opens the plant up to be infected with stalk rot.

Bacterial stalk rot. An unusual corn infection that occurs at ear height rather than coming from the soil. It is transmitted from overhead irrigation by water is sprayed from a lake, stream, or pond.

Barley stripe rust. A disease that affects barley. Yellow stripes with dots of orange pustules appear on plant leaves.

Barley yellow dwarf. A virus that barley can contract from aphids.

Base malt. During the drying process in malting a grain, modification is stopped by destroying the enzymes and dries out grains to about 4 percent moisture. At this point, the grains are considered base malt, the basis for fermentation of most beers worldwide.

Beard. A beard on barley refers to the 3-inch-long awn — or bristle — that projects from the top of the plant.

Body. A term used when describing the depth of taste of a beer.

Brown spot. This type of fungus can appear on the leaf blades, sheaths, and stalks. The disease will weaken stalks and cause them to lodge, and it will also destroy leaf sheaths.

Bushel of barley. Weighs about 47 pounds (21 kilograms).

Buttress/prop roots. On a corn plant, these roots close to the soil surface support the stalk.

C

Caramel or crystal malts. These add a sweet taste to beer and contain unfermentable sugars. These malts come in different degrees of roast and, therefore, color.

Caramelization. The process of applying high temperatures to decompose sugars in malts. This creates unique flavors and color in a beer.

Colony. A growth of yeast cells in a mass. Usually seen as discs in plates or a slick covering the surface of slants.

Common rust. Common rust looks a bit darker than southern rust, and the pustules are longer. Common rust will appear as rust clumps on corn leaves.

Conditioning. The process of adding a little priming sugar to the beer before you bottle it. The residual yeast will create carbon dioxide in the form of bubbles and a head on your beer.

Corn smut. One of the common diseases that can affect corn. In Mexico, people actually harvest this fungus — *Ustilago maydis* — and eat it. It can enter a corn stalk through wounds caused by hoes, insects, or other problems.

Couching. In the process of malting grain, once the acrospires have reached ⅔ of the length of the grain, the grain will be given a carbon dioxide bath to stop the growth process. This is referred to as couching the grain.

Cultivar. A specific species of plant developed through deliberate selection or breeding.

Cutting hoe. This type of hoe is suited for weeding. It is sometimes referred to as a push or Dutch hoe. These hoes have a sharper blade than the draw hoe because they are made for cutting weeds. The hoe is used differently than the draw hoe.

D

Diastatic power. The amount of starch conversion of a grain to produce simple fermentable sugars.

Draw hoe. The draw hoe is used when planting seeds as it creates furrows. It is called a draw hoe because you use it by pulling it toward you. It is great for breaking up compacted soil that makes it hard to plant seeds.

Dry hopping. The technique of adding hops after primary fermentation.

Dust-free box. This special box is virtually dust-free and, therefore, keeps sterile items sterile.

E

Ear and kernel rots. These types of rots are caused by the same species of fungi that cause stalk rot. This infection will decrease corn yield, and the seed is useless in beer production or as seed because the kernels have been too damaged.

Endosperm. The layer in a grain that surrounds the embryo of a seed and provides it with food.

Erlenmeyer flask. A conical-shaped Pyrex container capable of withstanding heat. Used to make pitch-able starters.

F

Farmers market. A meeting place of local farmers who set up booths to sell produce, plants, and even seeds from their garden.

Flail. This tool comprises a handle with a 3-foot-long, broom-handle-sized piece of wood that is attached with a leather thong to another 2-foot piece of wood. You use the flail to strike the head of the grain to release the grain.

Flaming. The process of sterilizing the openings of containers and their caps by passing them through an open flame.

Freon®. While not actually a gas, it is a product name that refers to any number of refrigerants called "chlorofluorocarbons."

Furrow. A small trench dug in the earth by a plow or hoe.

Fusarium head blight/scab. A fungal disease that bleaches out the color in the spikelets of barley.

G

Germination. The process in which the grain begins to grow shoots.

Germination room. Where grains are placed as part of the malting process for beers made at commercial breweries.

Glumes. The bottom of the bristly parts of the barley plant.

Gray leaf spot. Gray leaf spot will infect the leaf sheaths and leaf blades. It appears as long gray or pale brown lesions that are long and narrow and run parallel with leaf veins. These lesions are about ¼-inch wide and about 1 inch long. If the disease progresses, the lesions will grow together into long stripes and will kill the leaf, which will affect the yield of the plant.

Green malt. Barley that is placed in the germination room to begin the malting process.

H

Headspace. The area between the top of your beer and the top of the vessel.

Home brew. 1. (noun) referring to a homemade beer: "I just drank some home brew." 2. (verb) to describe the process of creating beer at home: "I have yeast, hops, and malt ready to home brew."

Home brewer. Someone who creates beer at home.

Hooded. A term for barley that means it has a short awn.

Hop yard. This is the place where hops are planted in a garden.

Hull. The outer protective layer of the barley.

I

Inoculation. The process of placing live yeast cells into growth media in order to increase cell production.

Inoculation loop. The tool used to move small amounts of yeast cells from one place to another.

K

Kiln. A large, high-temperature oven.

L

Lager malt. Lager malt is used to make lagers, which are usually a pale-golden color. Lagers usually do not contain any other roasted grains that would make the darker color often found in many types of ales.

Lodging. When grain falls and clumps due to wind and rain.

Lovibond. Refers to the color degree of a grain. The higher the number, the darker the grain. This helps a brewer determine the flavor, aroma, and color a grain will produce in a beer.

M

Maize dwarf mosaic virus. Corn infection in which young leaves will have light and dark mottled or mosaic patterns on them. Corn infected will have excessive tillering, multiple ear shoots, and poor seed sets. If the infection occurs early in the plant's maturity, it may develop root and stalk rots and die off.

Mashing. Done by adding boiling water to the grains. Mashing activates enzymes that break the starches released during modification into fermentable sugars. This is the process used to create pale-colored malts, pilsner malts, and malted wheat.

Modification. Process during which enzymes begin to break down the proteins and carbohydrates into simpler sugars, lipids, and amino acids and open up the starch reserves that exist to help the plant grow. The enzymes rip open this bag and allow the starch to be released.

N

Net blotch. A serious disease that can cause loss of yield. It is identified by its light-brown spots with dark-brown, net-like patterns on the leaves, glumes, and sheaths.

Nodes. This part of the plant contains the hop buds and will grow into cones that are used in home brewing.

Northern corn leaf blight. When this fungus attacks corn, it looks like tan to grayish-green, elliptical lesions that range from 1 to 6 inches in length on the leaves of corn. The infection begins on the lower leaves first, but does the most damage to the upper leaves. It can kill corn plants and gives a gray look to the leaves.

P

Parafilm®. This a wrap used in a laboratory to stop the drying of slants and plates.

Plates. These are sometimes known as Petri dishes. Plates work cultures in order to show if there is some sort of contamination and are used to test cultures to make sure they are pure.

Powdery mildew. Plant disease that can affect grains and hops as well. It resembles gray patches of fluffy fungus.

Primary fermentation. The beginning stage in brewing when vigorous bubbling caused by yeast transforms sugars into alcohol and carbon dioxide.

R

Rack. Process of clearing the beer off of the dead yeast called trub.

Rhizome. The name of the horizontal stem of a hop plant. A rhizome is planted underground, where it send out roots and shoots from its nodes.

S

Scald. One of the most destructive barley diseases that results in the highest lost of yield from a garden. This disease affects the sheaths, leaves, glumes, and awns of barley plant.

Seed rot and seedling blight. When a seed is germinating, fungi in the soil or hiding in the seed can attack it. Some of the species of fungi are Pythium, Diplodia, and Fusarium.

These types of diseases will kill a seedling.

Sheath. The leaf that grows under the head of the barley and covers it. On corn, these are the outside leaves you have to peel away.

Sheave. A bundle used to dry the grain before threshing.

Slants. Solidified wort-agar media has a large slanted growth surface that allows the maximum exposure to oxygen for long-term storage. Slants can be placed with a mother culture in a refrigerator and can keep for up to a year.

Southern corn leaf blight. This fungus causes sores or lesions on the leaves of the corn plant. They appear as long, tan sores that are up to an inch in length on the leaves that have brown bor-

ders. This fungus can destroy a corn plant.

Southern rust. Southern rust can be seen as circular to oval pustules and give the leaves that they infect a rusted look. These pustules are pinhead-sized and are full of orange spores that can be rubbed off a leaf. This rust can damage or kill corn.

Sowing. The process of planting seeds in the ground.

Stalk rots. These are caused by Diplodia zeae and Fusarium species of fungi. These infections will destroy a corn plant. If cold, leaf diseases, or insects have injured stalks; they are more susceptible to be attacked by these fungi.

Sting. Corn nematode that feeds on the outside of the roots, root tips, and along the sides of the roots. If untreated, the root will die. These types of nematodes are found most often in soil that is made of 80 percent or more of sand.

Straw. The straw is the stalk and head that is left of the plant after the grain is removed.

Stubby root. Caused by a corn nematode that feeds on the root tips. The damage they cause stunts the growth of the roots, hence the name. The result of the stubby roots is that the ears that formed on the plant are very small and underdeveloped.

T

Threshing. The process of removing the grain from the head of the plant.

Tillering. Extra offshoots on a barley plant that create a greater yield of grain per square foot.

Trellis. A trellis provides a support and a direction for hop vines to grow.

Trub. The sediment in the bottom of a fermentation vessel or sometimes in the bottom of a beer bottle.

U

Unfermentable sugars. Some of these malts undergo a special heating process that converts the starch in the hull into complex, yet unfermentable, sugars. They are unfermentable because they are still in a form that yeast cannot process.

W

Winnowing. The process of separating the grains from the bits of straw.

Wort. Term used for fermenting beer.

Wort media. Malt sugars mixed with nutrients in order to encourage the most optimum growth of yeast.

Author Biography

John Peragine is the author of 101 Recipes for Making Wild Wines at Home: A Step-by-Step Guide to Using Herbs, Fruits, and Flowers *and* The Complete Guide to Making Your Own Wine at Home: Everything You Need to Know Explained Simply. *He has been home brewing and winning national competitions for years with his beer and wine creations. When not writing, John plays the piccolo in a regional symphony and spends time with his wife and children.*

Index